Escape
to a Small Town!

Create a New Life
& Fulfill Your Dreams
in a Place
Where You Can Breathe

Lisa Rogak

Williams Hill Publishing
Grafton, New Hampshire

This publication is designed to provide accurate and
authoritative information in regard to the subject matter
covered. It is sold with the understanding that the publisher is not engaged in rendering legal, accounting, or
other professional services. If legal advice or other expert
assistance is required, the services of a competent professional person should be sought.

First Edition

Printed in the United States of America

10 9 8 7 6 5 4 3 2 1

Publisher's Cataloging-in-Publication
Shaw, Lisa Angowski Rogak.
    Escape to a small town! : create a new life &
fulfill your dreams in a place where you can
breathe / by Lisa Rogak. — 1st ed.
    p. cm.
    Includes index.
    LCCN: 99-90108
    ISBN: 0-9652502-2-9

    1. Country life—United States—Handbooks,
manuals, etc. 2. Urban-rural migration—United
States—Handbooks, manuals, etc. 3. Moving,
household.   I. Title.

    HT381.R64 1999   643
                         QBI99-311

Published by Williams Hill Publishing
RR 1 Box 1234
Kinsman Highway
Grafton NH 03240
603-523-7877
www.williamshillpub.com
www.movetothecountry.com

For Sharon

Contents

Introduction

What does it mean to live in a small town? Is small town life the last true bastion of a sane life in the United States today? Are small towns, from the rolling green hills of New England to the dense forests of Oregon, the last fragments of Eden that we have left?

Since I've been writing about rural life for the good part of a decade, I've corresponded with people all over the country who wish to exchange the pace of the city for the charm of small town life. However, I can't help but wonder, do they really know what they are getting into? Yes, nature is peaceful and quaint at times, yet it's easily transformed into an entity that's entirely different from the images you read about regularly in *Vermont Life* or *Montana Magazine*.

According to *Time Magazine*, more than two million people have moved from the city and suburbs to a small town from 1990 through 1997. Do they all know what they're getting themselves into? After all, small towns are fickleness incarnate, and beauty can quickly turn to ugliness. Lovely, winding dirt roads where children play with dust-covered dogs in fragrant August turn into furious mud bogs in springtime, swallowing up autos and shiny L.L. Bean boots without remorse. Four-wheel drive vehicles are wonderful tools, however they still slide off the road when brakes are applied on patches of black ice.

When you see a picture of a pastoral small town in summer, you are usually looking through the viewfinder of a skilled photographer. You see beauty incarnate; green fields, red barns, freshly whitewashed houses. What you don't see are the bugs that make it impossible to sit outside amidst all this beauty, nor do you see the hissing raccoon emptying the contents of our trash all over God's land. And you won't see the beer cans and empty potato chip bags tossed to the side of the road by harried summer vacationers.

If my tone appears harsh, I apologize. I am hard-pressed to think of a better life than in a small town. I've lived in a small town since 1988, and no other existence offers the kind of freedom, peace and beauty that small town living does. At the same time, you should be prepared for the reality of small town life because it is not always pleasant and tranquil. From a distance, a small town can look like Nirvana, a refuge where neighbors and everyday life appears more manageable than the chaos you deal with now. As I look out the window now I see a beautiful mid-winter afternoon, the bare branches of the oak trees glisten with a faint coating of snowflakes, and Mount Cardigan stands majestically outside my window, while Mount Cube, the beginning of the White Mountains, hovers just past Cardigan's right shoulder. I have not, however, forgotten what will happen in April when my four-wheel-drive vehicle will spend four hours trapped out on the road in a couple feet of mud. Such is small town living; one minute you adore nature, the next you are fighting it. The most successful transplants accept it and pitch in; after all, in a small town you won't find the bevy of municipal services available in a larger town.

So the next time you visit a small town where you

think you'd like to live, try to see it through a set of more realistic eyes. I'm not saying that you have to become negative, but it's always a good idea to work a little harder to see the not-so-nice things about the town you desire. This way, you won't be surprised the first time you are confronted with it after you've settled in.

As you read through the pages of *Escape to a Small Town! Create a New Life and Fulfill Your Dreams in a Place Where You Can Breathe,* keep in mind that you should try to apply the advice of myself and others to your own hopes and dreams about your own life in a small town. After all, what may have fit me like a glove may send you running back to the city as the result of an overdose of isolation.

The good news is you can find your balance in a small town, and balance is a rare commodity these days. It's out there for you. Take your time, and be realistic about your expectations about what life will be like for you in a small town. By the time you've finished reading this book, you'll be well-prepared to locate the place that will feel like home for you.

Lisa Rogak
Grafton, New Hampshire
pop. 900
February 1999

Chapter One
Getting Ready to Move to a Small Town

When I first moved to a small town in northern New England I hauled my TV along with me. Soon after I moved, however, I lugged it down to the basement. First of all, the reception from the 200-year-old valley cape I had moved into was lousy. This was before the days of pizza-sized satellite dishes, when a behemoth dish ran $5,000 and were still only sporadically spread throughout the state. We jokingly referred to them as the state flower.

But more importantly, I was too busy to turn it on. Before I moved to a small town, I imagined my life would be more leisurely than in the city, and I'd have more time to do the things I wanted to do. This turned out to be a myth: the people I know in my small town lead extremely hectic lives. I remember feeling surprised to learn that the rushed American way of life had spread to the seemingly bucolic small town I had selected. Of course, this feeling was contagious.

Despite my schedule, I discovered that one part of my life had changed since I moved to a small town: I no longer bought as much stuff as I did before, simply because I was not exposed to it on a daily basis, either through the television or the wide variety of retail outlets that are easily accessible in any urban or suburban area.

In the decade that has since passed since I became a small-town resident, this has changed somewhat, with increased retail and corporate development occurring even in my neck of the woods, but still it remains pretty low-key overall.

Eventually, however, I weaned myself back into the TV population by occasionally watching it at friends' homes. Why? Because I felt my life was out of balance, something I never thought would happen to me if I was living in a peaceful, friendly, small town. I had made the mistake of looking to the town to keep me from my demons.

And right now you may harbor fantasies of how the various sides of your life will fall into perfect balance once you move to a small town, but as it happened with me, you'll probably still have to work at it.

Over time, I discovered that living without a TV in a sparsely populated area quickly made me feel like I was *too* isolated from the rest of the world. Of course, the Internet has done a lot to change that; most of the people in my town of 900 are online, a fact that regularly surprises people from away, especially since there's nothing much in town except two general stores and a gas station. I initially moved to Grafton, New Hampshire, because it was the only place where I could find a house I could afford in the late 80s. As it turned out, the town was a perfect fit: Real estate is cheap because many people think it's too far for them to commute. As a result, many of the people here generate their own income, a fact I discovered only after I moved here. This is why I recommend you rent and not buy a house when you first move to a small town. There are so many parts of a small town that won't reveal themselves until you are living there full-time. You could find it fits perfectly, or that it was a horrible choice. It's better to know *before* you commit to a mortgage.

Setting Your Goals

Okay, so you've finally decided that you're going to move to a small town, security and salary be damned. What next?

What exactly are you going to do, how will you set your goals, and how will you know if you've reached them?

The only way that many of us know that we're getting anywhere is if we set regular goals and then reach them before proceeding to the next. Planning your move to a small town is no different.

The goals that you set depend on when and where you want to move, as well as what you plan to do for work or what kind of business you decide to start after you get there. Out of necessity, some of these goals are going to be tangible, while others will be intangible ones. For instance, you may say that you want to be living in a small town in western New York State two years from today, with a job that pays enough to support you while you spend time starting and then building up your mail-order garden supply business. These are tangible goals, and probably the ones that are foremost in your mind.

But say somewhere in the back of your mind you also think that your move will enable you to slow down your pace, probably drastically at first. The goal of relaxation is intangible, and frequently measured only when you look back and compare your new calmer self with your previously chaotic lifestyle that once seemed second-nature to you.

Undoubtedly, you'll have your own specific goals—both tangible and intangible—that you're interested in accomplishing, but use this checklist as a guideline to start to set your goals concerning your move to a small town.

First, get a notebook, and start to write in it daily, jotting down your observations and ideas about your new small-town life. Keep your notebook by your side as you read through this book. Write down whatever pops into your mind as you read. Start by writing the answers to the following questions. Try to go into detail about the *why* behind each of your answers:

- When and where do you want to move?

- What kind of work do you want to be doing?

- What do you need to do in order to reach these goals?

- If you want to see if your job will transfer seam-lessly from city or suburb to a small town, what kind of research will you do to find out before you move? What needs to be in place for you to make your decision?

- How do you want your life to have changed by the time you move to a small town? And what are the first few things that you want to accomplish once you're living there? In the course of planning your move, undoubtedly, *you're* going to change, whether it's having more focus or the satisfaction of reaching an important goal. It's also important to set goals for after you move to a small town in order to keep the momentum going so you'll keep your disorientation at bay, since you are essentially going to take on a lifestyle that in some ways, is totally new from the life you're living now.

- And finally, what do you see yourself doing differently in your life once you are living in a small town?

Every week that goes by, no matter how busy you are, you should plan to do something that will bring you closer to your goal of small town life, whether it's sending out a resume, checking out house rental prices in your dream small town, buying a book about how to start a particular business, or even taking a day or weekend trip to the area on a regular basis. In some cases, it may be pretty difficult to know in advance how quickly you'll progress with your plans, but if you can draw up a schedule in advance and match yourself up against it every week, you'll have a guide to follow and to tinker with as you proceed.

Hint: if you're like me and tend to drastically underestimate the amount of time it will take you to accomplish a certain task, do yourself a favor and overestimate the length of time it will take you to move to a small town.

What Kind Of Small Town Is Best For You? Part I

Just as one city differs from another, every small town that you'll encounter can be vastly different from another. The question you must ask yourself is, "What sort of small town do I want to live in?"

Many of us think of a small town as a bustling downtown made of pretty white buildings and corner lamp posts, quaint little coffee shops and towering church steeples filled with friendly people who wave as you pass by. Others see it as a plot of land surrounded by trees where the chirping of birds effortlessly mixes with the sound of the wind blowing. Some of us see green hills that look like giant emeralds, while others foresee a placid lake dotted with little fishing boats that make a gentle whirring sound as they move from channel to channel. There are different kinds of small towns and you must decide which one is for you.

If you wish to move to a place where people don't ask you to be on the school board or go to the church pot luck supper, if you would rather spend a day without hearing another voice or the sound of an automobile, then the cute little town with the coffee shop and corner lamp posts is not for you. Your wish is for isolation, which means you should consider moving into the outskirts of a small town. But you should be aware that if you are leaving a big city where screeching tires and loud boom boxes on every corner are the norm, the shock of complete silence may be more than you can take.

It's a good idea to take a vacation to a cabin in the mountains without a TV or radio and see how the silence affects you. Many people who live in noisy neighborhoods dream of being completely isolated from the human race until they realize that silence can be just as bothersome as noise if you're not used to it.

Likewise, if you think you'd like to live in a bustling village, make sure that is what you really want. The anonymity and impersonality that often accompanies city living will not be readily available in a close-knit small town. You may find the gossip and familiarity residents have with each other to be charming at first, but you should realize that if you show up at the general store in the middle of the day too much, rumors will start about how you don't work, or how you must live off a trust fund, and so on. Don't laugh: this happened to me when I first moved to a small town. It took time for people to get to know me before those rumors faded away. And even today, because I drive a 20-year-old Mercedes I bought for $1000 from a salvage yard, people in my small town consider me to be wealthy.

Be aware that since you are new in town, you will be talked about. In a small town filled with traditions, anything that's new or different will stand out. But at the same time, you should realize that most of these people lead very busy lives, and their days are not consumed with talking with you. It may even be scary to hear people talking about your cousin from Los Angeles coming to town just moments after you heard it yourself.

Don't be alarmed if none of these visions of small town life fit your ideal, because in a small town, nothing is black and white but instead is made up of many shades of gray. Another type of small town living is the happy medium between the two lifestyles described here. This is the kind of life where you can be as involved as you want or as solitary as you desire and it is all up to you. Certainly, this is the most appealing of the lifestyles because of the amount of freedom involved. The question is, how do you find this kind of small town?

When you start looking for your small town, try to find a place with much privacy yet relatively easy access to shopping, culture or whatever aspects of life are important to you. Achieving this happy medium depends on your ability to understand the community that you *think* you want to become a part of. Many small towns have a bureaucracy equal to city hall, so it may require taking a day off here and there to attend a planning or school board meeting. What this will do is allow you a look at the powers-that-be in the small town you are thinking of calling home. Once you get a feel for the people you meet, you will have a better handle on the kind of small town you are moving to.

What Kind Of Small Town Is Best For You? Part II

To define the different kinds of small town even more, and to help you to see that your fantasy life of living in a mountaintop cabin far from other humans may *not* be the best move for you, here's what one woman has to say:

"My husband and I have been investigating small towns in Maine, and have pretty much settled on the Portland area. Actually, not the Portland area, but Portland itself. We fell in love with the city and plan to spend a couple of weeks looking for an apartment.

"I guess we are just not boonies people. We like the city, we like apartments, we like being able to walk to things Just moving to Portland, Maine [from Hackensack, New Jersey] is like moving to a small town for us."

What this shows is you must decide just how far you are willing to go when you decide what kind of small town is best for you. In the midst of the screaming sirens, violence, smog and overcrowding that may be causing you to dream of more tranquil places, you could have a tendency to overestimate just what kind of small town you want. Just as a hungry person may have eyes bigger than his stomach, a frustrated city-dweller may wish for total isolation after yet another close call with a bicycle messenger while crossing the street. But making this sort of decision after something disturbing happens may lead to a kind of anxiety worse than what you think you are experiencing in the city.

Here's an example, as reported by a friend of mine who grew up in a small town in New Hampshire.

"My former neighbors moved to Salisbury, New Hampshire, with the best of intentions to make a whole new start in life. After all, they were getting away from it all and not looking back. They bought a nice lot adjacent to my own, built a beautiful contemporary home with second-floor balconies overlooking acres upon acres of birches and oaks. Our street is a quiet one and at night, the silence is almost eerie. This couple and their children lived in that home for six months before the silence got the best of them and they left their dream home and returned to the city. Isolation, at first very comforting and relaxing, can soon send the most ardent supporters of small town life blindly running back to the shelter of city lights and beeping horns.

"Although I did not know the couple well," he continues. "My assumption is that they would have been significantly better off choosing a town that had more to offer socially than Salisbury. There is only so much social interaction you can get from a trip to the general store for a coffee and newspaper."

This is what I mean by choosing a small town based on the fact that it is everything the city is not. I suggest you make a list of everything you enjoy about the city. Perhaps you love spending Sunday mornings at the cafe, listening to folk music and eating bagels. Maybe your idea of the perfect evening is taking in a play and dining in a fancy restaurant. Whatever it is that you love about the city, ask yourself if it is something you can live without, or live with on only an occasional basis if the nearest big city is two hours away. If not, it doesn't mean that you *shouldn't* move to a small town. What it does mean is that maybe you shouldn't move to a town that puts you in the middle of nowhere.

The kind of small town you want definitely depends on the number of things you enjoy about the city. If there really isn't a lot you enjoy about being in the city, and all you really want to do is enter a life of near-frontier living, then by all means, take the chance. But if you have not experienced living in solitude, and only *think* it is what you want, I suggest doing a little research. Rent a cabin for a week and choose a locale that is quiet, far from shopping malls and plazas, a spot where the light emanating from your neighbor's house is so far away it may as well be a star. Although a week isn't going to give you a definitive answer on whether or not you will be happy in a small town, it may give you a hint as to what type of small town you are looking for.

Finally, if what you hate about the city is the overcrowding, look for a small town on the outskirts of a small to medium-sized city. This may be *exactly* what you are looking for. Here, you'll find peace and quiet, but not utter and perhaps deafening silence, combined with the feeling of being away from it all, but where you'll still be close enough to it all to find a decent array of restaurants and shops. The benefits of being in the suburb of a medium-sized city is that many such towns are not automatically urban extensions of a major metropolitan area, but instead a smaller town with many of the cultural and social activities you may enjoy now.

Just as a warning, I have known many people whose main reason for leaving the city was to escape crime; as a result, they move to a house without close neighbors just to assure that they will not fall prey to crime. Soon after, however, the crime they put up with doesn't seem so bad and certainly no worse than the quiet and isolation of the hinterlands. For these people, I suggest the previously-described small town with a good security system, the best of both worlds.

The Three Kinds of Small Towns

I cannot stress enough how important it is that you shed most of your perceptions of small town living if you have not experienced it firsthand for an extended length of time. Your weekend hike in a small town, the one when you saw a deer walk right up to your door and you drank coffee in the fog of early morning, should not be your sole impression on which to base your motivations for moving to a small town. It's fine if an experience like this is what made you start dreaming of living a small town life in the first place, but if you drop everything and think that every day of your new life will resemble that weekend can get you into trouble.

Here, then, is a brief description of three categories that most small towns fall into. This can help you narrow your focus as to the kind of town you think you'd be most comfortable with.

A Drop Out Town

Living in this kind of small town will require at least a half hour to get to a major supermarket and shopping area. A Drop Out Town may not have its own schools; in a federated school district, several towns may share school facilities for budgetary reasons. A Drop Out Town doesn't have a real shopping district; instead, a general store or two, perhaps a gas station, and that's about it. Watch the early morning traffic. If there's no discernible outflux of traffic consisting of people who need to get to a 9-5 job, it's a good bet it's a Drop Out Town. And if people in towns that appear to be closer to "civilization" make fun of the town, then it's a sure bet for a Drop Out Town. Grafton, the town I live in, is a Drop Out Town. It has a population that hovers around 900 on a good day, with more junk cars than people, is at least 30 minutes from New London and Hanover, which are both towns with an abundance of shopping areas, several supermarkets, a college, and traffic lights.

Suburban Small Town

This type of small town has a concentration of houses and stores, and probably a true bustling village. One or more banks may have branches in the town. A Suburban Small Town often has several police officers and a paid town manager. Canaan and Enfield—the two towns that are closer to "civilization" than Grafton, is are both considered to be somewhat suburban small towns, Enfield moreso because the commute for most residents is shorter. There may be a couple of general stores in town, a hardware store, a couple of small restaurants, and at least one video store.

A Small "City"

This defines Lebanon—next to Hanover and Dartmouth College—to a T. Lebanon has been bestowed with the honor of being voted one of the 100 best small towns in America, in Norman Crampton's book by the same title. Lots of small businesses are able to succeed here, along with a superb reasonably-priced Italian restaurant, a mall, a large green, full-time library, community college, opera house, senior citizen center, and lots of shopping, especially in the western part of town, which boasts everything from a WalMart to a McDonald's to almost everything else. Lebanon serves as the major shopping area for people who live up to an hour's drive away or more, and is about 40 minutes from my house, which is why if you choose to move to a Drop Out Town, it's necessary to plan your shopping trips in advance. But the benefit to living in a Small "City" is that the true boonies are probably only five or ten minutes away. And even within a Small "City," there are true patches of country, though they can be comparatively expensive pieces of real estate for the area.

How can you tell which category the small town you have your eye on falls into? Usually you can do it by sight, but there are other ways to confirm it. One good way to tell is to get a copy of the previous year's annual reports. Again, using the example of my area, the town clerk in Grafton is a very part-time position; she gets paid only several thousand dollars a year. The town's full-time secretary makes about $15,000. In Canaan, which is the next town over with triple the population of Grafton, the full-time administrative assistant (notice the change in titles) at the town offices makes double what Grafton's does. Also in the town reports, check the difference in the budgets for committees like the library, historical society, and dump and/or transfer station. And check the hours of the library: in Grafton, the library is open three hours a week, an hour at a time, on Wednesday, and that's it! In Canaan, it's six days a week, nine until 6. But whether it's a Drop Out Town or a Small "City," it's highly likely that the largest single expenditure in a town's annual budget is for road maintenance.

Chapter Two
Scouting Out a Small Town

No matter how much you may want to drop everything and just move to a small town, you're going to have to do at least a little bit of homework in advance. The first step is to start to nail down exactly the kind of town where you'd be happiest. In a word, this means you'll not only have to figure out the specific things you like about a small town, but also what you don't care for.

Who & What to Ask Before You Choose a Small Town

The time to look seriously at a small town is *before* you make an offer on a piece of property there. Or at least before you've signed the contract. "Interviewing" a town is not difficult, bt it requires a lot of chit-chat and some seemingly casual questions to get the information you really want. Some of the hard facts are easy to get direct from the source, but the real feeling of a small town and the attitudes of the people who live there are more subtle and often simply have to be "nosed out."

First, the sources for facts on cost of living and other documentable subjects:

- Contact the area's Chamber of Commerce for an economic and demographic overview of taxes, education facilities, churches, housing, utility costs, etc. They have this information readily available for businesses thinking of relocating to the area.

- Call the town tax office for property tax rates. Be sure to ask if there are any special assessments, user fees or other charges levied separately and not part of the tax rate. In many small towns, the tax rate does not tell the whole story; sewer and water, flood control, even mosquito control may be separate charges.

- Once you have a particular piece of property in mind, it is worth a stop at the town hall to look at the tax maps and check the taxes on neighboring property that has changed hands more recently than the piece you are considering. If the town has not been reassessed recently, assessments are sometimes increased when a property is sold, reflecting the selling price.

- While you are in the town offices, ask for a copy of the previous year's town report. These have a wealth of information.

- Call the state tax department to find out what other state and local taxes need to be paid once you become a full-time resident there, such as income and sales taxes. Be sure to ask about county and local surtaxes, which in some states can add up to more than the state income tax.

- Call the regional office of the National Weather Service and get the real scoop on the local weather.

Even within a small state, weather can vary widely. There are rain pockets, places with constant high winds, etc.

• Look at the prices in the nearest large supermarket. Especially check those items you buy most frequently and would be most likely to purchase locally, such as food, cosmetics, medicines, household supplies, etc.   How far is the nearest full-service supermarket from the small town you are considering?

While these hard facts are the easiest to collect and evaluate, they may not be the most important issues in your decision to move to a small town. You need to learn about the way people live there, what they do in their spare time, how welcoming they are to strangers, and how their values match your own to evaluate how closely you and the town match. The fact that a small town is "standoffish" may suit you just fine if you value your privacy, while those who expect a constant social life would be very unhappy there.

• Begin at the village store, if there is one. A quick look at the merchandise they carry can tell you a lot about the tastes and lifestyles of your prospective neighbors. What kinds of wine and beer, natural foods, and other items are prominently featured on the shelves?

• Pick up the town newsletter or newspaper, if there is one, and read the ads and local news. What is happening in the town? What kinds of lessons can your children expect to find? Is there an active 4-H or scout program? Do the senior citizens have activities?

- Subscribe to the local or area newspapers, weeklies, leisure papers, etc. Pick these up in the grocery store, then call and ask to be put on their mailing list. (For free papers you pay only the postage.)

- Look for a bulletin board at store or Post Office. What events are advertised there, what services?

- If you are already looking at a house or property, ask the real estate agent as many questions as you can. Try to work with an agent who lives in the town you're considering. Listen for little hints: what may seem like idle chatter can tell you a lot.

- Even if you are not a regular church-goer, try to attend a service or two of the community church. It will tell you a bit about how welcoming the community is, since in many smaller towns, the church is one of the only regular meeting places.

- If you have school-aged children, visit the school. Ask the principal about the town and the activities for children there.

- Visit the town's library. Not only will the books tell you something, but the librarian knows a lot about the town and its residents—or at least those among your prospective neighbors who read. Ask about the town's history as a conversation starter.

- Stop in at any shops—antique, junk, gift, craft or whatever—and ask casual questions.

While you can't just pull into someone's driveway and begin interviewing them, you can be chatty with anyone who has a business. Don't say you are thinking of moving there, just pass the time of day and comment on how pretty the town looks, or ask what's likely to be on the menu at the firemen's supper, or if the town has an historical society—whatever it takes to start a conversation. To begin, pick up on some local phenomenon, issue or whatever interests you. Are the roadsides plastered with "Vote No on Question 3" signs? Ask the couple with the antique shop what Question 3 is. Does the little craft shop by the roadside have a well-kept garden? What about other homes in the town? Comment on the garden and ask the proprietor if there is an active local garden club. You may already have seen the signs promoting their annual garden tour, but playing dumb will give you a chance to start a conversation, and from there, you can move on to other subjects.

—*Barbara Radcliffe Rogers*

Playing Fortune Teller with your Future Small Town

How can you tell if the small town where you plan to make your dream home is all it's cracked up to be? More importantly, how can you tell if some big developer is planning to build some new development in your town or the next small town over?

Sometimes it's hard to get a handle on the future of a small town home, especially when your rose-colored glasses are firmly in place; after all, while you're still in the city or suburbs, it's hard not to look at your new small town and see nothing but the positives.

The simple truth is that, with a little digging, it's

possible to predict the future when it comes to development but also when it comes to figuring out what the people are like in your new town. First, the people:

Towns and states that start to become their own fantasies in your mind make it hard to find the cracks in the veneer. Even if your fantasies about what it will be like to live in your dream town are pretty tame by comparison, you won't immediately begin to see the downside of life in your new town until you've lived there for awhile. Remember the well-worn advice to keep your ears and eyes open and your mouth shut. It works for kindergartners; it will work for you once you move to a small town as well.

So how can you get some idea of the negative things about your new home before you move there so you know what to expect? It's not easy, and most of the negative stuff you hear in the beginning will probably be tales that result from long-fermented bad blood between neighbors and relatives in the town. But here are a few ideas:

- Start to hang out at the general store or other shop in town that's frequented by locals. Take most of what you hear with a grain of salt, but watch what the owners—not the hired help—do. Listen to what customers and staff are saying, and then ask the owners for their opinion. Everyone has a different view, but the owners tend not to gossip much, or else their business might go down the tubes. They'll be able to straighten out some of the stories for you, or at least covertly point out who's who when they enter the store. Don't be obsessive in gathering your information; rather, ask for it in an offhanded way.

- Open your eyes. Specifically, what does the town

look like? What do the houses look like and how are they kept? How many abandoned houses are there in the town?

- What are people talking about? Is there one particular issue that they tend to focus on for weeks at a time before picking up another and then running with it as well?

- Start reading the newspapers, both the weekly and the daily papers. In my town, the rift between the volunteer ambulance and fire squads is well-known in your area, with the squabbles sometimes garnering front-page coverage in the daily paper, while the letters to the editor, articles from both sides and the detailed selectmen's minutes appear in defense in the weekly papers, which will print almost anything. If something this notorious is going on in the small town you move to, keep your comments to yourself until you've been living there for a year or two. Ask questions, and be polite about it, but don't choose sides *yet*, even if someone asks you to.

Next, development. I almost bought a house a few years ago where the guy who owned the adjacent lot was planning to spend several years mining the granite out of it. Unbeknownst to me, the realtor didn't say anything—if she knew, that is—and if I were to look at the deed, I'd see an out-of-state owner whose ambitions I assumed were like my own: to have a place where I could relax. He even had a deeded right-of-way across my land. But I was so taken with the house and the land that I didn't bother thinking about it. And this was several years after I had moved to a small town.

Not everyone is going to be forthcoming about future development in your area. But you can get some idea by looking at the towns around you as well as your relative distance from them and the attractions in your town. And start by asking the following questions:

- Are you choosing a major tourist area that is already pretty much saturated with development? Has the town recently passed anti-development legislation? How much does an acre of land go for in the town's prime commercial area, as compared to an acre of land on the outskirts?

- When you look at a particular piece of land or house, who owns the adjacent lots? Does your land contain deeded right-of-ways? If you can, find out about the development potential of these adjacent lots. Are they held in the name of a corporation or individuals?

- Is there a major body of water in your town that acts as a magnet in the summer? Are any highway traffic deferment plans projected for the future, which may mean an increased number of cars past your house? Is it priced so high as to prohibit its purchase by locals?

- How far is your town located from major business centers, colleges, tourist attractions? The further away, the less likely that development will hit you.

- How have other towns in the area developed in recent years? Has there been a boom or bust? Is there any one individual who owns a disproportionate amount of land in town? Is there a conservation district in town? Is your land adjacent to it?

You'll undoubtedly think of other questions to ask based on your own area. What's important is that you do ask before it's too late.

How I Chose My Small Town

I had spent a decade in big cities: Los Angeles, Minneapolis, New York. There are good reasons to live in these places, but respectively, star-struck accountants, snowbanks in May, and sardine-packed subways, none of these top my own personal list. Over time, the big city's financial and cultural opportunities didn't seem as compelling as it once did. The assets were increasingly offset by the costs and hassles of getting through the average day.

When I started to fret or complain about the small and large miseries of city life, I found I could ease my mind and blood pressure with a single word: Vermont.

Vermont. Green mountains. Winding roads. Maple syrup. More cows than people. Country stores. Of course, that's the tourist's impression of Vermont. But so far I'd mainly been a tourist in Vermont. I'd been to the state to ski several years ago. More recently, I'd visited the state for work. That recent trip was what made me start believing that living in Vermont should be, and could be, more than a daydream.

In March of 1997, I spent two weeks in Johnson, Vermont. Johnson is a tiny town in Northern Vermont. It's near a major ski resort, but you wouldn't necessarily know that since it's not overrun with tourists or the trappings. There's a post office, a church, a country store, a few small shops, and an artist's colony near the main street. That's about it. Your car could whiz through it in seconds. Fortunately, I got to stay long enough to get a glimpse of the people and daily life in this town. I believe Johnson is quintessential Vermont, utterly charming without being pretentious. There are rows of worn but still grand houses and lots of buildings with inviting porches. One side of the town has quiet streets that lead to the woods, the other side inclines to a small university at the top of a hill, with a great view of the mountains. When my reasons for visiting Johnson ended, I didn't want to leave.

The annoying practical matters of life required that I return to the city's ball-and-chain, at least temporarily. And in retrospect I see that this was actually a good thing. As much as I enjoyed the peace of Johnson, I had renewed appreciation for all you could do and see in Minneapolis, my home before I left for Vermont, I began enjoying myself again in Minneapolis, so much so, as a matter of fact, that I got a bit confused. As the months wore on, I knew I still wanted to move to Vermont. But I also wondered if I had lived too long in cities to truly live in the country permanently. Perhaps a compromise was in order. Could a city in Vermont be the answer?

I tested this hypothesis near the end of 1997 by spending a week in Burlington, the largest city in Vermont. I looked at apartments, hung out in coffee shops and bars, wandered around the University of Vermont. I told everyone I met that I was thinking about moving to Burlington, told them why, and asked what they thought.

The people of Burlington were friendly and helpful, but after a few days and countless conversations, it became apparent that Burlington was not the place for me, at least for now. Vermont is one of the best preserved states in the country, but Burlington, once a sleepy college town, is growing rapidly. There are already a few large shopping centers, chain stores are moving in, and in the local papers I read about a number of large real estate developments in the works.

Burlington is the cultural center for northern Vermont, so certainly some would view these developments as signs of progress and economic opportunity, but not me. After years in the big city, I could only see a rising cost of living, crime, pollution, and traffic, in other words, the very things I was trying to get away from. I realized then that I was expecting the impossible, that one place could be everything for me. And sometimes when you want everything, you end up with nothing. My Burlington trip taught me that I couldn't have a country and city life in one place.

Did I then make a beeline for Johnson, Vermont? Actually, no. I'd also learned in the intervening months that northern Vermont was probably a bit too remote for me and my work. For the time being, I needed to have quicker access to Boston and New York. So I did some more homework, and visited a few more towns around the state.

A few months later I settled in a town a few hours south of Burlington, about the same size as Johnson. It also has a post office, a church, a country store, that's about it. Unfortunately you do have to drive one town over if you want real live cows, but I currently make do with milk and plentiful Ben & Jerry's from my country store. And like Johnson, your car could whiz through my town in seconds. Since I like the fact that most of those cars whiz right through, I'm not going to reveal the name, but I'll offer this hint: the town is near a river and borders New Hampshire, which ought to narrow down your search to about fifty towns...

Good luck on your path to finding your own ideal small town. I promise you the result is well worth the soul-searching and all the efforts.

—Derek Scheips

Flight or Fancy?

In response to my first book on rural life, *Moving to the Country Once & For All*, I received the following letter. The tone and content of the letter hit me, and so I decided to print it here, in a slightly edited format:

Dear Lisa,

We live in Silicon Valley, California, and want to move to a small town. We'd like your help finding places that fit the following criteria:

- In the U.S.:
- California near the San Francisco Bay Area (most preferable)
- Oregon
- Washington
- New Hampshire
- New York
- Massachusetts

- Small Town Atmosphere
- Clean air
- Clean water
- Open spaces
- No traffic congestion

- Trees
- Temperate climate

- **Good for a home-based business**
- Easy access and local calls to an Internet service provider
- Good phone service
- Existing telecommuting cottage industry
- Zoning for home-based business

- **Zoning**
- To control growth and protect from the nearby urban sprawl

- **Within two driving hours of**
- An ocean
- Skiing
- Camping
- A large city (say over 300,000 people)

- **Within half a driving hour of**
- A Unitarian church
- Hiking
- A university
- Alanon meetings
- Medical facilities

- **Within 15 driving minutes of**
- A good public or private school for grades 5 through 12 that can accommodate kids with learning disabilities
- A health club
- Hewlett Packard employment

- **Low cost of living**
- Low income, sales and property tax

- Inexpensive real estate
- Appreciating real estate prices

- Community
- Cultural diversity
- Some liberal neighbors
- Some libertarian neighbors
- Some sophisticated neighbors with advanced college degrees
- Tolerant neighbors
- Active parent participation
- Coop preschools
- Low crime rate
- Organic food supply

Okay, what's your initial reaction to the above list? People frequently send me detailed descriptions of what they envision their ideal small town to be, but up until I received this letter, I hadn't received a list as detailed and as unrealistic. I think these people would be more comfortable in a commune with separatist qualities or a quasi-suburban elitist development, since they want the best parts of small town living without having to ever confront what they perceive as the downside of small town life, which I interpret to be conservative neighbors, zoning that will let them do whatever they want but will restrict their neighbors from doing the things that these people wouldn't approve of, etc.

The letter made me angry. These people didn't have a clue about what they will encounter in the real world of small town living; they were looking for their version of Utopia. There are pros and cons to every community, and though it's possible to find a small town with some of the above attributes, the place that they're describing simply does not exist. *Anywhere.*

First, nowhere are you going to find an unpolluted environment. Even in tiny Grafton. On a broader scale, there is acid rain and clearcutting in the Northeast, mining in the Southwest, and similar problems in small town communities in the Northwest. And for someone who wants to avoid traffic congestion, these people seem to plan on doing a lot of driving. Oceans and skiing are not conducive to either few people or little traffic, last I checked.

As far as taxes and real estate go, you're never going to find the ideal situation, and the same holds true for jobs or a home-based business. And if you want good public schools, you're going to have to pay the price with your wallet.

I think the thing that bothers me most about this list is its exclusionary tone. They claim they want to be part of a small town, but their list of what they will accept in the people they associate with indicates that they have a bias against people who are not like them. Once in awhile, somebody calls me about small town life and to ask about certain small towns I prefer. In the next breath, he may say, "But I don't want to have anything to do with rednecks." All I can say is look, if you're going to live in a small town, you're going to deal with people who hold different beliefs than you and whose families have probably lived in the town you covet for generations. They are as educated as you, albeit in a different vein. The advanced degree that these people speak of will not get them very far in a small town. After all, you can't jumpstart a car, thaw your pipes, or impress or earn the trust of your new neighbors with a piece of paper with a few capital letters printed on it.

Don't set yourself up to be knocked for a loop. And don't expect to find the advantages of a city in a small town. You may move to a small town that has a small town/western bar—and not much else—and it may take a day before your road gets plowed after a big snowstorm. This is small town reality. The good news is you'll learn to revel in it.

How to Move Your Kids to a Small Town

Kids aren't furniture that can be loaded onto a van and moved to a new house. Any move requires some special attention to the needs and fears of children, but when the move involves a change of lifestyle as well as location, those needs grow even greater. And the older the children are, the more difficult it is for them to pull up roots.

The time to begin thinking about how to make a move to a small town a truly family event is almost before you even start thinking seriously about scouting out new towns. That doesn't mean that you should necessarily tell the kids that you're contemplating it before you've given it serious thought, but it does mean you should be thinking about the part they will play in it.

Just as you can't change overnight from being a city or suburban person to a small town kind of person, neither can your kids. Both you and they need a little preparation in order to make a smooth and rewarding transition to small town life. Perhaps if you put your-self in their junior-sized shoes, you can better picture what it will be like for them.

- While you have many years of life experience, which includes a great many successful changes, to draw upon in imagining how a change will affect your life, children do not. Their perspective is based on a much shorter and probably less varied experience. So any change at all, will be a greater change to them.

- While your life is made up of a great many facets, the life of a child has few basic components: home, school, family and friends. A move uproots them from 75% of these.

- Your excitement over the prospect of living in a small town may sustain and support you through some of the stress of the move; your children probably do not have these same goals or expectations. You can help them to share your eagerness, but don't be surprised when it doesn't spring full-blown.

- You have been thinking about making this change for a long time before you decided to do it, whereas your child will probably learn about it as a part of your well-developed plan.

- The adventure of a move to a small town may capture your imagination, but children are basically much more conservative than adults. Change for the sake of something new does not appeal to them as they tend to take great comfort in the familiar.

How and when should you tell them? Obviously, the younger the child, the easier a move to a small town will be on them. Preschoolers will pretty much tag along, since their lives have not developed the patterns of school and friendship that come later. School-age children develop deeper ties as they advance in grade. Depending on your children's ages, it may be a good idea to prepare them a bit before you announce the plan. If your child's life has been primarily urban, begin by planning weekend and vacation activities in a small town. Choose things that your child enjoys to do and watch for interests that can be encouraged, such as camping, hiking, nature, animals, or outdoor and individual sports.

Once a child has activities to look forward to, it is easier for them to look forward to a small town as a place where they'll be able to do these things more often. Riding a horse, canoeing, cross-small town skiing, ice skating, mountain climbing, or having a rabbit can be just the incentive a child needs in order to look forward to moving to a small town.

The degree to which you involve your child in making decisions about the town and house you will all eventually live in depends both on the child and on you. Be careful taking a child house shopping, however, since a little thing that you may not even notice may have a big effect on them, since they will not be making the decision themselves. In our own experience of moving to a small town, our young daughter was terrified that we would move into one house we looked at because a bird had been trapped in the house and she found it dead in the room that probably would have been hers. On the other hand, a child who is brought into the process and given some input into the final result will tend to develop a greater interest in the move and not feel so helpless in the face of it.

Not all the following will fit every situation, but these tips are offered by parents who have moved successfully with their children:

- Prepare them in positive, not negative ways: Choose "In our new house in a small town we'll have a barn for you to keep some of your sports equipment in," instead of, "Before we move you'll have to get rid of a lot of the stuff in your room."

- Don't extol the joys of gardening and other small town projects too much; to most kids, they spell one word—work. Find pleasant activities to talk about that are more in tune with their interests.

- Let them take *everything* they want to take, even if you know they will throw it away when they get there. All of those things are part of their security, and by moving to a small town, perhaps in a different part of the country, they will be giving up enough that is familiar.

- Suggest that they decorate their own room in the new house, even if they choose the most garish wallpaper in the book, and then stick with it, no matter what it looks like. At least their room will look like they want it to.

- Go to the child's new school—without your child the first time—and get suggestions from the prospective teacher. Ask if one or more classmates can begin corresponding by email before the move so your child has a friend there.

- Be sure your child has a chance to meet the teacher before walking into the classroom for the first time. If the school is one where students change classes, be sure your child has a tour of the school before the first day there.

- If possible, get your child involved in some organization before the move, so that membership can be transferred. Scouts, Camp Fire Girls, 4-H or other club will give them a familiar program. If you move during the summer, this may provide an opportunityfor meeting other kids before school starts.

- Invite a close friend from home to visit for a week, especially if you move during summer vacation.

- Be aware of your child's social dynamic—how they make friends, how they see themselves in relation to others, whether they are leaders or followers, whether they are shy or confident. Your understanding of their perspective will help you support them during the move and help them make new friends.

Remember that a move from the city or suburbs to a small town is changing your child's entire life—home, friends, school, places to play—and that in your child's eyes, it is forever.

—*Barbara Richmond Rogers*

How to Find a Job in a Small Town

If you check out the help-wanted websites, newsgroups and mailing lists on the Internet, you'll find that a small but significant number contain listings for jobs in small towns. In addition, there are many magazines and newspapers in small towns that post their entire classified and Help Wanted sections online, and many of these posted positions can be performed on a freelance or contract basis, which means, of course, you can move to a small town without having to secure a new job there first. And of course, most corporate web pages now list employment opportunities as do state, regional, and private employment placement services.

In addition, there are many places that offer up profiles of businesses in web directories as well as on a company's own web site, you can make sure it's the kind of company you'd like to work for in the first place. One way to search for businesses in a particular small town is to go to a search engine and type in the name of your dream town or area plus the word *employment* or your field of interest. If you find a particular company near your prospective home send a resume to the director of human resources, or even stop by to visit the next time you're in the area to check out future job possibilities.

Here are a few more job hints:

- If the area you're looking at has a local business publication, send for a subscription, even if it's primarily a vehicle for badly-written press releases. The paper will provide valuable information about area businesses, new incorporations and trade name registrations, as well as news about company expansions and job promotions, the better to get your foot in the door.

- Also check out Pro CD (www.procd.com). This is a CD-ROM that lists more than 12 million businesses nationwide, complete with address, phone number and type of business. The listings are compiled from the phone book and chamber of commerce membership lists and you can type in an industry code, town and state to see what comes up.

- Company ProFile, offered by Information Access Company, gets a little bit more specific. Although this CD-ROM lists 150,000 private and public companies throughout the United States, you can request a list, for instance, of the top 100 companies dollar-wise, industry-wise, or state-wise, which will give you some idea of a company's pecking order within a state.

- There are many more options for small town employment than can be listed here, both online and off. Use your instincts and don't be afraid to contact a company with no current job listings.

Keeping Your Job When You Move: One Woman's Story

Donna Cunningham has been an employee at AT&T Bell Laboratories, based in Murray Hill, New Jersey, since 1980. She's held a couple of different jobs at the company, but in 1989, when she met the man who would become her husband, she was working as a global media relations manager for the company.

She had assumed that when she married her husband—a Vermonter who couldn't fathom moving to New Jersey—that she would have to leave her job. "I told my manager that I loved working for Bell Labs, but a six-hour commute wasn't going to work," says Cunningham.

"To my surprise, my director said he had to find a way for me to keep my job, and it didn't take long, because we looked at the fact that I already had a computer at my home that was supplied by the company so I could work at home and read my e-mail on the weekend."

When they decided that Cunningham could do her

job from 400 miles away, the company also set her up with a videophone, a two-line cordless phone, an answering machine, fax machine, computer printer, company email account, and modem. This allows her to easily work with the department secretary who's back in the New Jersey office. "If I need to get certain things done, I just fax or email a note to her," says Cunningham. "When she finishes it, she just faxes or emails it back to me. Otherwise, I wouldn't know that it got done, but we have everything in writing and it's very convenient.

Cunningham says that it took no time at all for her to adjust. "I had been doing so much electronically anyway on the phone or by e-mail that I don't even think that many people realized I was not physically in the office," she said. "People realized after awhile that I had moved, because they noticed that when they returned my call they were calling another area code."

However, she adds that there were people who didn't know that she had moved until two years later. If a reporter called Cunningham's New Jersey number, the secretary would transfer the call to her up in Vermont without a hitch. In fact, some of her co-workers usually had her number, but they sometimes didn't realize that things had changed. "In fact, some people at the labs still think I'm in New Jersey," she laughs. "Sometimes they notice that the header on the email or fax is different at the top, and that's when they'll say something."

To maintain contact, Cunningham goes into the office once or twice a month, and she stills attend conferences, flying out of nearby Burlington, Vermont. She says that some of her colleagues also work at home, but only for one or two days a week. "They always call me the ultimate telecommuter," she says. "But I just think that I'm just a little farther down the hall than I used to be."

She says that one instance where her telecommuting is a disadvantage is when it comes to keeping tabs on new developments in the labs. "It's a little harder for me because I can't just bump into somebody in the hall," she says. "When I'm in New Jersey, I'll go down for a couple of days for a meeting or media visit, I'll stay an extra day so I can go in and spend time in some of the labs just so I can get an idea what things look like. I like to meet with people in person and find out what they're doing, or meet with the whole department and let them know I want to hear from them if something new happens."

She says that when she started working from home, telecommuting was nothing that was really radically different at the company. "We've always had an informal sense of telecommuting here," she says. "If you had a need, you just did it. The supervisors always felt that if you have something that requires concentration and quiet, and if you don't need to be in the lab, you can certainly do it from home."

Cunningham says that she's had an overwhelmingly positive reaction from people, whether it's co-workers or press contacts who call her for information. "Frequently, reporters will call late at night or on the weekend, and they apologize for calling, but I never mind helping them at that time. At AT&T, we all put our home phone numbers on all releases and advisories that we send out to the press. The advantage that I have is that I already have everything there at home to do it," she says. "I can even fax out documents as I'm talking to the reporter. If I was still in New Jersey, I would have had to go into the office to first get the paper and then fax it to the reporter."

Cunningham's first bit of advice for people who want to telecommute, then, is to work for a company that supports telecommuting. "It makes a difference to work for a company that cares about its employees," she says.

And it also helps if you have a great office space to work in. Cunningham's husband built and designed their house—he's an engineer and also works from home—and he knew that they'd both have their offices here. He designed the first floor of their three-story house with this in mind: 1/4 of the space is her office, 1/4 is his, and the rest is a living space with a sofa, TV and VCR. Cunningham says it's convenient because whenever she needs to review a videotape for work, she can do it right there in her office. And she likes to work with her golden retriever by her side, who she considers to be her coworker.

Though she's always been comfortable with her job responsibilities, she's not sure that a person could just walk into any job and do it from a remote place right off the bat. "For instance, if I have to talk to a reporter and tell him what a particular laboratory looks like, I'd better know what it looks like," she says. "I have to be very knowledgeable about the company, and I'm not sure you could get that information if you were telecommuting full time from the beginning. I don't need to go to as many meetings as before, though I do regularly teleconference myself into some of them either with a videophone or a regular phone."

She says that the company is not losing any money because she's telecommuting; in fact, she says, they're breaking even when it comes to expenses. Back in 1989, when she and her boss made the decision for her to telecommute, they figured out that the overhead for an office at corporate headquarters is about $9,000 a year. "So instead of providing me with an office and lights and heat, we decided that I could use that money to buy airline tickets to fly down to the office," says Cunningham, who, except for her phone bill, pays for the utilities at her home.

"Sometimes I talk to people who say they would like to work this way, but that their companies won't let them," she says. "To me, that seems shortsighted on the part of the company. They'd have happier employees, and save money besides."

Her motto about telecommuting is the following: "The biggest difference between working here and in New Jersey is that a power lunch is taking the dog for a walk."

Chapter Three
Laying the Groundwork

Okay, you're getting closer. You've started to investigate the pros and cons of several small towns, you've begun to sniff out a number of employment opportunities. And you now know the kinds of things you'll need to do to keep your family happy before, during, and after your move.

Next on the board is to ask yourself the kinds of questions that most people who move to a small town never ask themselves. The issues of renting a house or apartment in a small town or picking the best time of the year to move may seem a little nit-picky, but it's better to explore all of your options now, before you make a major change in your life, than later after you've uprooted yourself and your family and you never thought to ask the landlord whose responsibility it is to plow the driveway or bring your garbage to the dump.

Old House or New?

Once you've made the decision to move to a small town, the next choice you'll have to make is where you want to live, specifically what kind of house or apartment. The chances are good that you may have to search for awhile before you come across the right home for you. Considering the current real estate market in many small towns across the United States, you'll have a large number of homes to choose from with a great variation in positive and negative qualities. Large or small, extravagant or conservative, old or new, in the village or out on a back road, a small lot or at least 40 acres and a mule? One of the most important factors to consider when buying a house is whether you prefer an old house or a new one. There are pluses and negatives to both and all of the advantages and disadvantages and they should al be weighed carefully.

To begin with, let's settle a general standard of what is an *old* house versus what is a *new* house. Now, here in the Northeast there are still many houses that are 200 hundred years old or more that are completely inhabitable. What you consider to be an old house also depends on your own personal definition. I know someone who considers a house built only 15 years ago to be an old house. To be fair, let's designate any house built more than 30 years ago to be an old house. Since there has been a significant amount of construction done in many small towns across the United States within the last 30 years, this seems to be a reasonable time period to use as a gauge.

One of the very basic considerations you should look at if you're considering buying an old house is the structure of the building. Old houses were built to last. They were built with more time and care than the majority of houses built today, and they tend to have heavier, more solid frames. If you find an old house that has been well maintained, chances are good that its frame will be strong. However, if it has developed leaks, look out because you may run into rotting timbers and expensive repairs.

You should also check into the history of the house. In many old houses, there may at some point have been a fire that could have weakened the frame's integrity. In a new house, chances are excellent you won't find rotting studs or fire-weakened walls and that the materials used have been approved for local building standards. What you might run into, though, is a more sloppily put-together house. As home construction has become a thriving small town industry with people who have started construction businesses on a part-time basis in order to make some money, a certain percentage either don't know what they are doing or they try to cut corners whenever possible, or both.

In any case, in comparing the differences, you may find that a newer house feels flimsy. The walls feel thin, one part of the floor upstairs may sag when you walk on it, or the house isn't settled square on one corner of the foundation. Cutting corners produces weak spots that will magnify as time progresses.

Another important factor in deciding between a new house and an old one is the insulation. You need to consider the kind of insulation the house already has or if additional insulation needs to be installed. As a rule, an older house tends to have less insulation than a newer home. With an old home, a time-tested method of insulation is to replace the screens with storm windows every fall and tack a continuous sheet of plastic around the base of the house, as well as any unused doorways. Even with these precautions, an older house will still be a little cooler than a new house would be. A new house will probably have double-paned windows and blueboard insulation around the foundation with a very high insulating value. More and larger windows will also take advantage of the sun and its heating potential, which brings us to the issue of light.

There is usually a big difference in lighting in an old house as compared to a new house. Old houses tend to have fewer and smaller windows with more wall space. The rooms are very distinctly divided with a doorway between them. In a newer house, you'll find larger windows and probably more of them. Newer houses also tend to be more open, with expanded spaces and living areas that blend into one another. As a result, the existing lights are more often used for decorative purposes.

Plumbing is another issue to help you make your decision between old and new. The plumbing in older homes, although well-thought out as far as layout is concerned, may bring problems. Old pipes may burst and drains may clog due to years of residue buildup; toilets may need to be replaced as their mechanisms can fail. In a new house, chances are good your pipes won't burst, but you may run into other problems-- clogging or freezing, for example--if, again, the plumbing was carelessly designed or hastily put together. It may seem like I'm concentrating on the negatives here, but the positive aspects of both old and new houses is that plumbing can function well for many years if well-maintained and designed properly.

Another aspect to the old house/new house debate is project potential. If you think you'd like to make some improvements or changes to your house, there will probably be some differences between the work that needs to be done to an old house and to a newer home. Old-home improvements may require larger projects like reroofing, reflooring, resanding the floors, or slapping up new wallpaper. If you are motivated and have the time, these projects could be your cup of tea. While a new house probably won't need as many repairs, you may have some improvements in mind that will make the house more appealing to you. They include adding a deck to the back of the house, stencilling along the sheetrock to create the impression of trim along the tops and bases of walls, and adding some more cupboards in an extra space in the kitchen. These projects are not as time-consuming or extensive as those in an old house, but they'll make the house more your own.

I've mentioned some of the more important details to think about when considering an old house or a new one. Other factors such include price, taxes, and your desire for space, but are less vital components to considering the purchase of a house depending on its age.

When to Move?

You've found a small town that seems like a perfect fit for you, picked out a home, found a job, told everyone in the world that you are leaving the rat race for more peaceful days. Before you wrap that first wine glass in newspaper, however, you should think very seriously about the best time to move.

- Many people naturally pick summertime to pack up the U-Haul and head for the hills. Yet moving to a small town is quite different from just changing apartments in the city. Aside from favorable weather, summer is not the most opportune time to settle into a community. Small town summers are filled with fairs, picnics, festivals, and so on. In short, people are very busy. Once you show up at a summer function, there's a chance that you will simply fade into the throng of visiting relatives and tourists.

- Fall may seem like an ideal season to move. It is not. Veterans of small town living—at least in northern climes—do not see fall as the season to go leaf peeping and apple-picking. They see autumn as the road to winter—a time to brace for a replay of the blizzard of 1978 and to make sure the wood is split and the chimney is clean. Once again, the problem of fitting into the community arises because everyone else is so busy.

- Winter, as you may expect, is commonly thought to be the worst time to relocate. People are cold, unhappy, suffering from cabin fever, and praying for spring. Roads are icy, snow is piled high and pipes are freezing, yet winter is certainly not a throwaway season for the person heading for a small town because there is simply no better time to purchase a house. Prices are lower and owners are more eager to sell. Do not, however, purchase land in the winter since it is difficult to know exactly what you are getting into. Save your land shopping for the fall.

- Spring, with the constant rain and mud season, may be the sloppiest time of year but it's a great time to find your place in a small town. People are so relieved that snow has melted in favor of the bright colors of spring, that they tend to be just plain nicer. They are preparing for the summer fun and will more than likely tend to stop by and invite you to the town's summer events. Of course, some communities are friendlier than others, but in general, people will be quite open to new residents after the last snowflake melts.

Buy or Rent?

If you're like many people who dream of life in a small town, the real estate pages had a lot to do with your current odyssey towards a small town, right? You were on vacation in Vermont, Maine, or Montana, and you grabbed one of those ubiquitous real estate shoppers. The low prices! The old houses! The chance to live where and how you want!

Many people who make changes and move to a small town based on emotion, not planning, end up making big mistakes, for the most part. And buying a house that may turn out to be totally unsuitable can be one of the biggest.

Before you get tempted by that wonderful new contemporary house or ancient Cape, take a deep breath. I'll tell you why it's better to rent first when you decide to move to a small town.

Reason #1: You may not like it there

Yes, in your mind it's probably a lot better than where you are now—especially if a local told you that nobody ever locks their doors—but the house you will buy on emotion will probably be a lot different from the house you buy after you've been living in a small town for a year or two. By that time, you'll know a lot more about houses in general—after all, most urbanites' experience with home maintenance involve picking up the phone to call the super—how small town life affects houses and your attitude towards them, and—most importantly—if that particular town is a good fit or not.

When I first moved to northern New England, I moved to Barnard, Vermont, one town north of Woodstock, where I rented a house. The first couple of months, I thought I was in heaven. Then, dealing with the relentless crowds and traffic in Woodstock's tourist aura started to get tedious. This wasn't why I moved to a small town.

So I moved twenty miles across the Connecticut River to Lebanon, New Hampshire. I actually moved *seven* more times over the course of five years before I moved back to the town where I felt most at home. You probably don't have the luxury of doing as much "research" as I did, but once you're at least living in the area you prefer, then you'll be able to learn about the surrounding communities, and whether they're better for you than the first one you landed in. One other thing: real estate moves a lot more slowly in a small town than in the city or suburbs. You don't want to make the mistake of buying a house that might take you years to unload should you change your mind.

Reason #2: The isolation may overwhelm you

Right now, you're probably in love with the idea of getting as far away from other people as possible. Five miles out on a dirt road? Love it.

Stop! You're inviting a severe case of culture shock that may make you end up hating small towns. Ease into small town life, perhaps by first living in the village, or maybe a half-mile from the town center. I've discovered that if you move way out on a dirt road, it will be harder to get to know other members of the community—even though you're sick of people, you do want to get to know your new neighbors and to feel as though you fit in. If you're that far out, they'll figure that you want to be left alone, and will treat you accordingly.

Reason #3: The house itself

Hauling wood may seem like the bee's knees to you now, but although most people who do move to a small town do go through their pioneering years of cutting and stacking wood, and other accoutrements of rustic small town living, this lifestyle, and even these few rugged chores will wear thin after a few years. It's happened to me, as well as to more than a few people I know. The problem is that once you're tied to your home you'll need to deal with expensive home improvements--like a new furnace--if you want to live any differently.

Because I was renting, I was able to try out a number of different small town lifestyles before I committed to one. Now I live in a brand-new house of old design, with a fireplace that I probably won't use for at least five years (I'm still recovering from burning four cords of wood in my old place last winter) and a state-of-the-art forced-hot-water heating system that also heats our hot water. No splinters, no burned fingers, and I get heat at the simple turn of a dial. The road to the house gets rutted, muddy, or icy, depending on the season, but so what? I won't have to move again, all because I tested out a number of different towns and houses before I bought a house in settled in a town.

Renting in a Small Town

A few years ago, when I was researching the book, *Moving to the Country Once & For All*, I received the following letter. I thought it accurately conveyed the experience of going from renting an apartment in the city to renting one in a small town, so here it is:

"I'm planning to move to southern Maine next summer. I currently live in New York City: enough said.

"I'm going up to Maine this weekend to find a place to live and go on a few job interviews. I'd like to know if you have any advice on finding a quality, affordable rental in an area that has no apartment buildings. Are there any unknown channels? Do you deal with landlords any differently in a small town than you do in the city? What about rental agents? What would be the best way to land a rental in as little time as possible? If you rent a house, is the landlord still responsible for basic maintenance and repairs, the way he is in an apartment building?

"I'm also a little nervous because I've been living in big apartment buildings my whole life where things are pretty anonymous and the landlord is just some guy you send the checks to. The majority of rentals that I've seen advertised in the local Maine paper are in someone's home—and I've heard some wacky stories about living in that kind of proximity to your landlord. Also, the idea of living without a superintendent on the premises is a little foreign to me.

"Help!"

My response:

"I think in your case what you don't know is scary. Even in New York, I lived in the only apartment in a single-family house. Up here, it's the norm. One of my good friends is my former landlord a few town away. I lived in an apartment attached to her house right on a lake, and most every morning I would go downstairs and hang out and talk with her in her kitchen. It's a lot better, because you have access to your landlord, who can also introduce you to a lot of the stuff about your new area that it would take a long time to discover.

"You should check the small local newspapers, and not necessarily the daily paper, like the *Portland Press Herald*. Pick up the weekly giveaway papers. If you can gain access to the local college and hospital housing offices—I've had to sneak in the past—or email or check web pages for towns in the area, it's a good way to find out. And look at the bulletin boards at general stores in the towns you're interested in. If you know anybody in Maine, ask them to keep an eye out for you.

"When you first get up there, it will take you awhile to get used to the lack of anonymity that is endemic to New York City (for good reason, of course.) This was the thing that took me the longest to get used to when I moved to a small town. But don't assume that these people are nosy; they're interested in you and naturally friendly, or at least most of them are. So keep this in mind and try not to flip out. To answer another question, landlords are responsible for major and minor repairs. You can call on them in the same way that you'd call on your super.

"I don't think there are any unknown channels to finding an apartment. Spring is a good time to be looking, before things fill up for the summer, and depending upon where you are, before schools go back into session. Most realtors in small towns do handle rentals, but for houses only—not apartments—and probably because they've been on the market for a few years and haven't sold yet. Whether you work with a realtor or explore on your own, you shouldn't find it too difficult to find a place to rent in a small town.

Renting From 3000 Miles Away

Your city days are bleeding you dry and all you know is that if you don't move to a small town, you're going to lose it. But how are you going to rent a house or apartment when you're a couple of time zones away?

Your very first step should be to subscribe to a newspaper that covers the area that you hope to call home. This will provide you with a somewhat objective view of the area as well as listings for rental properties in the classified ads. You should also call at least one realtor in the area. Usually a realtor can supply you with fact sheets and exterior pictures of the properties in question, as well as information about the towns you're considering. They'll also know of properties that will be coming up for rental in the near future. Once you have taken these two steps, your options of what to do next branch out.

If at all feasible, your best bet is to use up some of your vacation time and spend a few days in the small town you'd like to move to the most. Even if you can only stay a couple of days, the trip will be worth it. Since small towns, like cities, have their good and bad areas, though to you, at this point, they may all look wonderful, the only true way to tell is by visiting. Once you set up dates, start planning. Make all of the necessary appointments ahead of time, if possible. Ask your real-estate agent to help you put together a schedule that will make the best use of your time.

You'll certainly want to take the time to wander around the town and visit the town hall and any other places that may help you to make your decision.

For many of you, however, spending a few days in the small town where you hope to rent a home or apartment is not possible. If so, you have several options. One is to have a friend in the area visit possible rental sites and provide you with feedback. At least this would prevent you from renting a house or apartment blindly. If you do not have someone to be your eyes and ears, you must work closely with a real-estate agent. Work with her over the phone and through the mail. She'll ask you a number of questions about the type of house or apartment you're looking for, and send you listing sheets and photos. After you flip through all of the listings and photos, there may be several properties that you find more attractive than the others. At this point, request color photos of the interior of each apartment or house, if your agent hasn't already provided them to you.

Best of all is if your real estate agent can send you a 15-minute videotape of the entire property, inside and out. If you can narrow down your possibilities list to just a few properties, videotaping should not be a problem. You'll then be closer to making your decision.

Chapter Four
Narrowing the Field

Okay, so you're starting to get answers to some of your questions. You've made a plan, you've decided approximately where you'd like to live, and have received some positive feedback from some of the employers you've contacted.

All that's left to do is to set a target date and start putting the pieces in place so that you can start counting down to the day when you'll start living the kind of life you know you were destined to live.

But you're not quite there yet. You want to make the move, but you know it will be a different kind of life complete with surprises good and bad, and while you know you're going to be happy living in a small town, the truth is that you're used to your current life.

In other words, you have to make a big change in your life, and you're not sure that you're ready.

Why Do You Think You're Stuck?

Some people know exactly when they're going to move to the small town of their dreams, the house where they want to live, and what they're going to do for a living once they get there.

They're in the definite minority. Most of you know you want to live in a small town, but beyond that, you're not sure of anything...only that whenever you do spend time in a small town, it's like pulling teeth to get you to head back home.

If you want to get more specific in terms of when you'll move to a small town, you'll have to first take a hard look at the various aspects of your life that you currently view as obstacles. Which can you handle with ease? And what is the number one reason why you think you are unable to move as soon as you would like to?

If you're like many people, the lack of a job is the primary factor holding you back from aggressively pursuing a move to a small town, or at least the belief that you won't be able to find a job that pays well and is challenging. Stop right there: do you know this is indeed true? Or are you just going by what you *think* is true? The first thing you'll need to do is to determine the kind of money you'll be able to earn in your dream town, based on the research you've already done. It may be less than you're earning now, but you already know that many of your expenses will be reduced, as well as your stress levels, and that leisure activities in a small town are not driven by money but by community.

So get a hold of the Help Wanted section in the local paper of your dream town. If all you see are burger-flipping jobs, don't fret. You can investigate job possibilities online, but for the real scoop you should call a personnel agency in the area—you've already ordered a copy of the phone book for your dream town, right?—and tell the counselor about your background and the type of job you're looking for. The agency is more likely to give you the detailed information you're looking for, because, after all, they do get paid if they are able to find you a job and help you move there. The agency may have some other ideas for you as well. It's also a good idea to check out the local office of the state Department of Employment. Most state employment agencies list job openings at America's Job Bank (www.ajb.dni.us).

Okay, this is all well and good, and you know you'll be able to find a decent job, but you're still holding back. Another fear may be that you're not sure where you want to settle. As I've described, you're going to have to take the time to learn about the towns that are definite possibilities, and then analyze them to see how they'll fit. For most people, this will involve a combination of reading about the area through local publications and more importantly, visiting the area. From now on, resolve to devote your vacation time to exploring likely candidates.

However, perhaps one of the major reasons why you haven't moved to a small town yet and haven't made concrete plans is the fear of change. If you've never lived in a small town before, the open spaces, complete darkness at night and people who are more friendly than you're used to might be a few of the reasons, plus the idea you've built up that your life will look totally different.

If this is the case, the first step to take is to make a list of the ways that your life will be different when you move to a small town, but also the things that will remain the same. Include the various aspects of your job, transportation methods, and leisure time. You may be surprised to see that there will actually be a number of things in your life that will stay the same. This new view may give you the impetus to start working on your plans in earnest.

The important thing to do is to take some action now so you don't feel like you're permanently stuck in a life in the city or suburbs that you're not wild about. If you start ticking off one item at a time, you'll feel you're that much closer to moving to a small town and it will begin to seem less like the impossible dream and more like the kind of life that you'll be living within a reasonable amount of time.

Moving to a Small Town 101

A woman once asked me how to really prepare to move to a small town. I knew she wasn't talking about renting a moving van or notifying the phone company, or other mundane tasks. She wanted to know how to alter her state of mind so that she can get a headstart on calming herself down so she could thoroughly appreciate life in a small town before she moves.

I told her to take it slow. Consciously try to reduce your pace of life. It may be difficult at first, but the first step is to become aware of it.

Here are some more suggestions:

- Eat a meal that consists solely of food that puts up a fight: artichokes, mussels, lobster, etc.

- Read the classifieds from back to front.

- Listen to an entire CD with headphones without doing anything else.

- Strive to be second.

- Stop at rest areas and actually *rest*.

- Allow that car to cut you off. Smile instead of

cursing.

- Unplug your microwave for a week and dig out your old cookbooks.

- Climb a tree and stay there until people come looking for you.

- This summer, go to a pick-your-own strawberry field, plop down between the rows of berries and then eat everything you can pick within arm's reach.

- Order in dinner for a whole week.

- Sit in a bubble bath and stay there until all the bubbles disappear.

- Take a sick day when you're not sick, but pretend that you are and stay in bed the whole day.

- Don't plan your next vacation. Schedule it as usual, and then figure out what to do when it comes.

- Make appointments with yourself to do silly things and then don't break them.

- Skip the escalator or elevator.

- Let your kid do something that would take you a fraction of the time to do—and then leave the room and do something to relax.

- Stop for yellow lights.

- Take off your watch.

- Instead of making instant pudding or opening a can, make the type that takes 20 minutes to cook. Or better yet, make it from scratch.

- Let that pint of designer ice cream thaw on its own without the microwave. Then eat it with an espresso spoon.

- Or, let it sit for two hours, then sip it with a straw.

- Take a guided bus tour in the city where you live.

- Eat an entire Chinese meal with chopsticks. No cheating allowed.

- Eat an entire Italian meal with chopsticks. No cheating allowed.

- Instead of setting the clock ahead, set it five minutes slow.

- Do one less than is expected of you.

- Don't iron. See how many comments you get. Ignore them.

- Take a day trip and go off in the car by yourself and do all the things that you want to do.

- Call a friend you haven't seen in awhile and sit in a coffee shop and devour pot after pot of decaf until you close the place down.

- Spend two hours of quality time with your cat or

dog.

- Write a letter by hand instead of typing it. Send it by regular mail.

- Cut the grass with a hand mower.

- Cut the grass with a scythe.

- Or, just let it grow.

- In a grocery store, find something that's been misplaced and put it back where it belongs.

- Parents: Just sit there and watch your kids as they play. Don't read or think or do anything, or tell them what to do. Just watch. Savor the moment and tell yourself to remember it.

- Stop work in the middle of a crisis and make a cup of cappuccino. Then close your door and sip it slowly.

- If you usually save time in a restaurant by not having dessert, or feel guilty if you do eat it, then have it first.

- Learn to whittle, or teach yourself another craft that uses only hand tools.

- Sew a dress by hand.

- Build a house of cards.

- Work as a model in a life-drawing class.

- Listen to music you grew up with headphones on.

- Spend the day at a historical recreation museum to get some perspective on how frenzied your life really is.

- Throw rocks into a pond. Watch all the ripples and wait until the pond is completely still before throwing in the next.

- Next time you're in a small town at night, pull over on a road with no lights and stop the car. Let the blackness and silence engulf you.

An Intermediate Step: A Small(er) City?

Clare L. Mannion, now a real estate salesperson in Santa Fe, spent fifteen years in Chicago before she finally left in 1991. She enjoyed living in the city and loves to go back to visit, but she views her move and her new life in Santa Fe as part of a process of change that had to happen.

In Chicago, she managed a hotel and also ran her own marketing consulting business, but she started to discover that as she worked longer hours and was more successful, she liked it less and less. She decided to make a move because she was ready to make some major changes in her life by balancing work and leisure more equally in a place that didn't require as much energy to live as Chicago demands.

"We all go through changes, but it's very difficult to change gears in your own environment," says Mannion. "I started to become dissatisfied with my work because I had been doing it my whole life, and if

I wanted to do something different, I believed I had to move. It's the same thing as going to a spa and losing weight: it's easier to go away to do it because the same stimuli are always back at home, making it harder."

She also felt that in her circle of friends and business colleagues, it would be difficult for her to scale back her life to the point where she would be happiest. "When you get negative reinforcement for change, it makes it very hard to do," she says. "When you are very successful at an early age, but you don't want to do the same thing any more, it sends shock waves throughout your community. No one quite knows what to do because it rocks the vision they have of their own world." She says that people around her didn't understand her motivations for why she wanted to change her life, and therefore didn't offer up a lot of support.

Though it was scary to make the change, she's happy she settled in Santa Fe. "There's a lot more personal and professional freedom and diversity that's supported and encouraged and almost demanded here," says Mannion. "I don't feel that was the case in Chicago. I spent a lot of time with people like myself in Chicago, but in Santa Fe, there aren't enough people for those many pockets to exist. As a result, you bump up against people with different and varied backgrounds here, and I think that's wonderful."

What she finds most appealing about Santa Fe, however, is the ability to mix work and play and to be wholly supported by the people around her. "In the winter, I can come to work in ski clothes one day a week, get in my car at noon, drive to the ski area that's fifteen minutes away, ski for three hours, and then come back to the office to work," she says. "In Chicago, if I wanted to do this and was working in a big corporate environment, I'd probably say that I'm going to a meeting and change into my ski clothes in my car."

Since she sells real estate in Santa Fe, she deals with many people who have moved to the area from elsewhere. She adds that these transplants tend to be in their late 30s and 40s who are beginning second careers once they move. "The fact that a lot of people in Santa Fe came from other places makes them much more open and welcoming towards new people, since they remember what it felt like to be new." They also tend to be physically active. "This is a four-season community, and people aren't lying around by the pool doing nothing," she adds.

For others who are looking to move to a place where they can better integrate their lives, Mannion has some good advice. "You should pick a place that feels physically right to you, because not all of them do," she says. But she adds that you'll need to be ready to take some chances and rely on your gut instincts, because if you wait until you find the perfect place, you'll never get out. "I spent a lot of time in Chicago trying to figure out what I would do once I got here," she said. "It's possible to have some idea of what it would be like, but you can't know until you get here. For me, nothing was the same. I went from walking to the corner to catch a cab to a 40-story office building to living on a dirt road and driving to work in a four-wheel drive vehicle with a dog in the back."

Though she loves her new home, Mannion does admit to missing some things about Chicago. "Sometimes I miss the energy of a big city," she says. "Santa Fe is a small wonderfully lazy little town, and it's very different from the energy of Chicago. I also miss the ethnic neighborhoods and being anonymous in a familiar place, and being able to walk down Clark Street without seeing a single soul I knew."

"I also had to give myself permission to miss things," she said. "Every morning for 18 months it felt like I was going on a blind date."

But in the end, she's glad that she moved. "One of the compelling things that was helping me to make my decision is that if I didn't make a change based on what my gut was telling me at that moment, I knew that I might not be able to do it in the future, because I'd lose my courage to do it," she says. "But because I've done it once, I'd definitely do it again. I could go anywhere now."

Another Intermediate Step: Buying A Second Home

Maybe you want to test out an area by living there part-time at first. Buying a second home makes sense. Planning to rent it out once in awhile makes even more sense.

According to the 1990 census, almost 8 million Americans own a second home; it's estimated that this figure will double by the time of the Year 2000 census. Indeed, new construction for vacation homes increased from 50,000 annually in 1994 to 75,000 in 1997, according to the National Association of Home Builders.

Why the great interest? Indeed, the combination of low interest rates, high stock market returns, and ironically, a manic focus on work all mean that second homeownership is a necessary option for city and suburban dwellers who accept that the only way to leave work behind is to physically get away from it all. The tax breaks—recently sweetened by the Tax Relief Act of 1997—which include hefty rewards on both mortgage deductions and capital gains, as well as the potential rental income, are the icing on the cake.

Today's breed of second-home purchasers tend to use their homes more often than those ten years ago, who viewed them more as a strict investment. If you plan to test the waters of a particular small town by purchasing a home there, if you want to visit regularly you should make sure that it's not so far away to dissuade you from traveling there on a regular basis. The happiest second homeowners travel no more than 150 miles, or four hours, from primary residence to second home. And if you expect to rent out the home for at least part of the time you're not using it, its location should be able to pull interested renters from your like-minded neighbors back home.

As with your primary residence, you should always invest in a professional house inspection to know what you're getting into. Keep a cool head and remember that you will be responsible for maintaining the place; you want to be forewarned about any major repairs before you sign the papers.

When it comes to securing a mortgage for your second home, keep in mind that the first thing that a banker looks at before approving financing for a second home is a lower overall debt-to-income ratio. Usually, the loan-to-value restrictions are similar to a mortgage on a primary residence—currently, 10% down payment is standard—but you should think twice about including projected rental income as part of your mortgage application. If you do, most lenders will then view the second home as an investment property, which usually requires a larger down payment *and* a higher interest rate.

This doesn't mean you can't rent it, of course. If you buy your second home with an eye towards renting it as much as possible, you'll probably be able to cover most—if not all—of your expenses.

But before you sign a purchase-and-sales agreement and commit yourself to two mortgage payments each month, you should be clear on how much time you plan to spend at your vacation home, and which seasons you'd prefer to be there. Sure, the rent you'll pull in from renting the home for July and August is good money, but will you feel gypped if you pay the mortgage for this home and can't use it in the summer months?

If you're working with a real estate agent, try to keep mum regarding your plans to rent the home. She may try to paint an overly rosy picture of the local vacation rental market to entice you to buy a slow-moving house. Instead, call second homeowners in the area who advertise their rentals in the local newspapers. Yes, the going rate for rentals may be $2000 a week or more during peak season, but how long does peak season last? Two weeks, or two months?

Sometimes it's difficult to be realistic about potential rental income; both realtors and sellers are both guilty of fudging the figures. But new second homeowners can also be unrealistic about the amount of rental income to expect. Many second homeowners don't figure in their own use when projecting rental income. For instance, if you want to use your second home between Christmas and New Year's Day, you'll lose a week during the peak season of the year in many ski areas.

If your second home is located in an area with a glut of rentals to choose from, you may want to invest in a few amenities so renters will pick yours over another. Hot tubs, saunas, and a satellite dish are currently popular.

Unfortunately, while these items may increase the rentability of your home, they are not tax deductible. The same deductions for your primary home—like mortgage interest and property taxes—apply to your second home as long as you can show that you used the home for more than 14 days each year, or for 10% of the time that it is rented. Plus, you're not required to report the income to the Internal Revenue Service, so the money is tax-free.

If, however, you rent out your home for more than 15 days each year, you'll need to pay tax on all rental income, but you'll also be able to deduct all of the expenses connected with being a landlord, from classified ads to housekeepers. In this case, deducting mortgage interest and property tax is tricky, because you're only allowed to deduct the interest and tax you pay for each day that the home is rented out. It's a good idea to keep a journal with brief daily entries in case the IRS raises its eyebrows later on.

If you buy a second home today knowing that you'll want to sell it in a few years, the Tax Relief Act of 1997 has had a massive influence on the tax implications of owning and selling a second home, and can be employed in two ways. First, if you live in your second home for two out of the five years and purchase another residence within two years, you can exclude $250,000 of the gain from the capital gains tax; if you file a joint return, the exemption is $500,000.

If, however, you use your second home less often than that, and you want to sell it after holding it for at least 18 months, the maximum capital gains tax rate you'll pay is 20%, which is a significant drop from the previous rate of 28%.

However, you shouldn't count on tax advantages or on the appreciation of the price of your second home as a given, or as the main reason to buy, since second homes are much more vulnerable to economic fluctuations than are primary residences.

The most important thing to keep in mind about buying a second home is to buy it for your own use and pleasure first, and second as a true investment. And if you don't plan to keep it in the family, and want to sell it one day, you should look first at the house and the view and location you want, in other words, the reasons why you bought the house. When it comes time to sell it, these are the same reasons why the *next* person is going to want the house.

Analysis: Get Me Out of Here!

Lora Sasiela is 28 and living in Manhattan, where she's working on her graduate degree in social work. She grew up in Queens and considers herself to have a city sophistication. Ten years ago, her mother and father moved to a small town in Maryland, and whenever she visits them she starts to think about what it would be like to live in a small town, too.

"It's created a contrast for me," she says. "When I walk around the town with my mother and she knows everyone, I love it. Then I come back to New York and I can feel my guard go back up, and I become aware of how much energy it takes to just walk around the city."

She plans to move to a small town when she graduates from NYU, and there are a few factors that control her decision as to where she can move. She would like to go into private practice as a therapist, but the insurance reimbursement requirements differ in each state; in New York, a therapist must be in practice for 6 years before the insurance companies will reimburse her, while in New Jersey and Connecticut the requirement is a fraction of that.

Other requirements: she'll probably do some post-graduate work in Topeka, Kansas, and wants to be close to a college town so she can benefit from an intellectual and cultural mixing of the minds. She doesn't plan to work in New York after graduation, and she is also concerned that the hinterlands she finally chooses to settle in won't have much in the way of food choices. "I'm very tied into the New York food scene and the gourmet shops, and I'm worried that I'll be limited in terms of what I'll be able to find," she said.

Her major fear about moving to a small town is that her support network and friends are all in New York. "The thought of just picking up and moving where I don't know anyone is very intimidating," she says. "How do you start building up that new net-work of friends? Which functions do you go to where you can meet new people?"

The analysis: The pros: Lora has awhile to plan her move; she's also open to a variety of different areas, and she's not tied down. "I don't have a significant other," she said. She mentioned that she thought about doing what a friend did, who recently moved from New York City to Woodstock, New York. "She had spent a lot of weekends up there, so she already knew people there, and she also knew what to expect," she reported.

The first thing she should do is to contact the state psychologists' association, or even a regional group, if it exists. To find such a group, you should call the state mental health association. You'll want to find an area that already has a number of therapists in private practice—to prove a need exists—but not too many, so that you'll have enough work. Scouting out college towns for the social scene also makes sense in terms of starting a practice, since it's likely that you'll be able to work with the college health department to get student referrals if the staff psychologist is overburdened.

The kinds of towns that would fit Lora's criteria contain state colleges or small private colleges with a population of under 1000 students. In New Hampshire, for instance, Henniker, with New England College, and Plymouth, with Plymouth State, both are very livable towns that bustle when school's in session. Dirt roads start less than a mile out of town, and there are movies every night along with a number of good restaurants. Stay away from towns like Hanover, New Hampshire with Dartmouth, or Burlington, Vermont, with seven colleges. You may have to struggle in a private practice for awhile since many people in an area like this who moved there for college and then stayed after graduation are competing for the same market.

Also, look at the Yellow Pages: If a reasonably small area has several columns of therapists, then that's too many. You could also call up a handful of the therapists listed and ask them about the prospects of an additional practice in town; if you specialize in a certain field and the therapists often need to refer other patients for special needs or to handle the overflow, then they'll be inclined to help you out in your search and get you settled. If the first therapist you call rebuffs you, keep trying. Some people see anyone who's remotely related as a big threat, even though the general consensus in a small town—no matter what your field—is that there's room enough for everyone.

And in these small college towns, the schools

welcome the participation of the locals. Some even offer free or greatly reduced memberships to the gym and sports facilities, and adult education classes on a wide variety of subjects. Once you meet one person in this network, you'll have access to many more in the community, and you'll probably be welcomed with open arms.

When I first moved to northern New England, I drove back down to New York every few weeks and stopped at my old haunts to stock up on bagels and cold sesame noodles, and then told the one person I knew in Vermont to invite all of her friends for a big party. That's how I started to meet new people while dealing with my urban withdrawal. And though the food in a college town may range from pizza to falafel, there are usually a few more elegant places in town which offer more sophisticated fare. Also, usually within an hour or two of a small college town is a larger city, with a wide choice of food, whether you want restaurants or gourmet shops. Chain supermarkets in small towns probably offer a wider variety than your small dingy city supermarket; in your decision to move to a small town, this should be the least of your worries.

How I Moved to a Small Town: Joan Paterson

The hardest obstacle I had to overcome in fulfilling my dream of moving to a small town was my fear. I had made the decision that I wanted to live in a town with fewer cars than people, and escape the smog and noise of the urban Bay area around San Francisco. I was determined to make a lifestyle change. I didn't have to worry about schools as my kids were on their own, I had decided to freelance so I could move anywhere that had access to Federal Express and UPS, and I had saved enough money to cover renting a place to live, my health insurance, and food bill for one year.

My track record for changing my life was pretty good. I had gone back to school as a mature student and graduated with honors, and I had been hired by a company that provided me with benefits like paid vacations and retirement plans. I had also bought a computer and learned how to use word processing and spreadsheet programs. Surely I could accomplish my goal of finding a small town, moving to it, and living happily ever after. Even with all this, I still had fears.

I knew how to research different towns and learn about the important issues in an area, like the crime rate, where to shop for groceries, how far to lakes and streams, the location of the nearest movie theater and library, and if a town looked like it was economically on a downswing. But underneath the rational layer of research, planning, and weeding out what not to take, was an underground pool of doubt and terror.

What if I moved to a small town and didn't make any friends? How would I feel if neighbors ignored me? What would I do if my car broke down at night on a rural road? How would I cope if I got cabin fever in the winter? Could I uproot and find another dentist I trusted or a store that sold dark roast coffee beans?

After living in California for over 15 years, I had begun to miss winter. I had even joined a figure skating class to spend one afternoon a week in an indoor rink to feel cold air against my face as I skated around. This longing for cold influenced my decision to move to a small New England town. My choice of town in New England was made easier by the fact that my son and his girlfriend were living in a town in central Maine. (Another fear: What if all the towns were Stephen King towns?) The area has an international flavor, judging by the names: Peru, Mexico, Madrid, Berlin, and China.

For a few years in the Sixties, I had lived in the town of Lachine in Quebec, Canada. The town was named for a French explorer who was searching for a route to the Far East in Canada and believed he had reached China. He called the town "La Chine." I had spent several good years there with many happy memories, so that is how I decided to move to China, Maine.

How did I dispel my fear? A few months before my move, I attended a workshop on personal growth in California led by Rabbi Steven Fisdel. When it was over, I told him of my plans to move: how I had reached a decision about where to live, how to earn money, and how to combat loneliness with e-mail. I also spoke to him about my fear.

His advice? Ignore them! He was right. When I stopped worrying about my fears, they stopped bothering me. I was able to focus my energy on the relocation process: deciding what to take with me, what to sell or give away, what to store. I rented a storage space, contacted a moving company, found a tenant for my condominium, and wrote a letter of resignation for my manager at my job.

My son and his girlfriend were living in a huge old farmhouse and were willing to rent two large downstairs rooms and a bathroom to me. We shared the kitchen, living room, and garden. When I settled in, I explored the nearby town of China and read the local newspaper for rentals. On December 1st, I moved into a cottage on China Lake, complete with dock where, I was told, the local newspaper was delivered by boat in the summer. I jumped at it!

What happened to my fears? I left them behind me! In their place I have new friends, neighbors who wave and stop to chat when they walk by, and a reliable mechanic to repair my car. A nearby town is hosting an international film festival this summer; two universities offer drama and guest lecturers; a local store sells coffee beans from around the world. And to reach all these indispensable places, I drive by a pond with two Canada geese and their five goslings. From my kitchen I see green fields and wooden post fences. Cows and horses, chicken and sheep line the road between my cottage and the nearest convenience store. Loons call in the cove just beyond my dock at night.

Chapter Five
Adjusting to Small Town Culture

You may be crackerjack when it comes to four-wheel drive on a dusty backroad and be able to build a barn or storage shed in a weekend with your bare hands. But if you are not well-versed in the politics and culture of a typical small town, it's going to be difficult to feel like you're part of a community, which is a big reason why so many people crave life in a small town these days.

So in some ways, you're moving to a foreign country. Take this into consideration when you initially begin to deal with the people who live there.

Getting By

Sometimes I'm not good at following my own advice. Though I do spend the majority of my waking hours working, I technically don't fall into the typical Type A paragon of American corporate life, but at times I do get so busy that it seems that I put more hours into my work than those harried corporate slaves I read about who are juggling every minute facet of their lives. No, I get into a jam because I simply love everything I do and have a hard time believing I am unable to do some of it due to time constraints.

A few years ago, I was feverishly working to bring in several projects on deadline when forces conspired to bring it all to a dead halt: one weekend, I had no water. The next, I had no power, which meant that again I had no water, since the pump needs electricity, and then the next week, one of my old-lady city cats died.

I'm not going to say, well, all this rushing around isn't exactly what I moved to a small town for, is it now? It doesn't apply, since I'm now working four times as long and hard as I did back in the city, though the first five years of my life up here did resemble a kind of sabbatical in some ways. But the events of those last few weeks all conspired to create for me what a friend calls a moronic convergence: suddenly, you become aware of what a moron you've become. Why are you doing everything you're doing? Are you happy this way?

Awhile ago, a friend and I drove to a diner in Rumney—30 miles away—for breakfast. I saw a couple of vehicles with Massachusetts plates in the parking lot, and once we were inside, I set about matching the occupants to their cars. As I watched people leave the diner, I saw my matchmaking instincts were on target. They all looked just a bit more polished, their clothes newer, their hair cut every four weeks on the dot. And I know why they do it: Because everyone else does the same thing where they live, and they'd be ostracized if they didn't. Of course, there are people up here who follow the same path, but they're few and far between. There are more important things to worry about in a small town, like figuring out what you're going to do until you get your water and power back...

However, there is sometimes an element of *Us vs. Them* where I live, as is the case in many small towns, and people on both sides react differently. I sense a bit of humility from the out-of-staters I meet, as they're thinking, "Oh, you're so lucky to be able to live here."

I've always possessed a harsh view of what most people consider to be their reality: Why spend three hours a day commuting to a job you can't stand just so you can come home to a house you can't afford and toys in the yard that serve only to tell your neighbors that you're in the same dire predicament that they are?

I'll admit this worldview developed because I grew up in Bergen County, New Jersey, where I saw ample amounts of this behavior. As a typically cynical adolescent, I pondered the energy wasted on these seemingly useless pursuits. I always possessed a sixth sense for the truth whenever people went out of their way to tell you how happy they were, when it was quite obvious that they weren't, so this kind of stuff jumps out at me today. The UPS man and Federal Express guy have both seen me in my ratty flannel pajamas (I've always worked from home), and though I don't begrudge anyone spending money on something that gives them a lot of pleasure, to do it for other reasons has never made much sense to me.

What would you do if your salary was only $20,000 a year, but the proportion of your regular expenses matched the decrease in income? For instance, if the $200 a week of miscellaneous money you have now was cut to $40 or less? Or your rent or mortgage actually was only 25% of your income? And your local entertainment options were mostly free and community-based? How do you think your life would change? Picture this: you're living in a small town that you love, the nearest mall and large-ish city is 50 miles away, and you only work 40 hours a week. How would your personal downsizing seem from that perspective? I know that everyone who wants to move to a small town does not fall into the category of overworked corporate peon, but most people tell me that the one factor holding them back from assuming the kind of life that they know they'd prefer is the reduction in income.

I moved from New York City to northern New England in March of 1988. Back then, I was living a life that's very different from the one I'm living now. I was living quite comfortably on about $15,000 to $20,000 a year. And before you say, yeah, but I was by myself, I know of families who still live on this amount, and they're able to live well by relying more on their abilities, efforts, and community with other people and less on the power of money. After all, there are worse things than living a life you're thrilled with on less money than you're used to.

Networking in a Small Town

Once you've actually moved to a small town, you'll suddenly face a new set of obstacles to overcome in your social and personal life. You may wonder how you're going to go about accomplishing this or that goal, or joining a particular aspect of the community. Many people move to small towns from a city and all of a sudden they feel isolated. They can't see or hear their next-door neighbors, there aren't many places to go or things to do at night, and they seldom run into people walking down the road. After you move to a small town, you may wonder how to interact with other members of the community.

Networking within a small town may seem difficult, especially for an outsider, but it really isn't. Although the locals may seem standoffish and reticent at first, once you gain their confidence you'll probably find them open, warm and loyal. Neighbors will stand by you in a pinch and look out for you even if they don't know you, once they've grown accustomed to your presence.

How do you go about making these connections, and what benefits will you reap? One of the biggest forms of networking is found by attending local social gatherings, and one of the most important and regular social gatherings in a small town is the church. Churches in small towns are still, quite frequently, the primary hub of activity and an excellent place to meet a wide variety of people. Even if you don't belong to a particular denomination, you should still go since most churches stage a regular roster of suppers, events, bazaars, and a variety of community service activities. You'll find the people there friendly and outgoing, grounded in their convictions, and very interested in you and your family.

Once you attend a few of these, the people you'll meet will be more than willing to answer questions, give helpful hints, and help out with big projects you have tackled. Other small-town gatherings include suppers held by youth groups, community dances, theater productions, and band performances, fairs, and auctions or flea markets. Some of these may sound odd, but you'll start to bump into more and more people with the same or similar interests and ideas as yourself.

Joining various community groups is another way to network, including fraternal organizations, historical societies, and business groups. Participating in a community dance group, theater or band is a great way to get in with an arts-oriented crowd, and if you join the historical society you'll meet people whose families may have been members of the community for generations. If you want to help people, small towns are

always looking for good reliable people to serve on the
volunteer fire department or ambulance squad, or to
help out when the Red Cross sets up shop for community blood donations. If you become involved in one of
these three activities, it's a good bet that you'll quickly
gain the admiration and respect of community members.

Kids are a great way to develop new relationships
in your new community in a relatively short period of
time; you can help out with school activities or volunteer some time in the library. If your child plays sports,
consider becoming a coach or help with fund-raising
activities. It's a good idea to make an effort to get to
know your child's friends' parents.

One aspect of small town life I would suggest you
avoid in the beginning is getting involved in the
political arena. Trying to become a selectman or member of the school board will inevitably set up a wall
between you and other members of the community
who have lived there longer than you have, perhaps
their entire lives. Chances are they'll view your en-
trance into political life as an attempt to turn the town
into the kind of place that you escaped from. Now,
you may have the best of intentions and may want to
help solve some very real problems in the community,
but the view that locals will take is that you don't
know how things work and you moved here to get
away from what you left behind, so don't fiddle with
the government in your new home, at least for the first
couple of years. Go to the meetings and voice your
opinions and work on grassroots activism, but don't
try to run the show to begin with. You'll only run into
coolness and resentment.

All of this networking will help in the long run.
People will start to wave to you when they drive by or
will stop to talk when they see you at the post office. If

you've got a problem, whether it concerns your garden or your plumbing, if someone hears about it, you can be sure they'll offer some advice. But you'll still have the chance to express yourself and the influences that have shaped you from years of urban or suburban living. Many people in small towns are more open to different cultures and eager to learn about the outside world than you might believe, so don't be shy about the possibilities of expanding their horizons; just be sure not to preach.

Once you've moved to a small town, get out and experience it full force. Hiding at home will get you nowhere and folks will think that you just want to be left alone. You have to make the effort to open the door and then you'll see your new life become tremendously richer. Making the connections with other people in your community as soon as possible will help establish your network to help you get through any foreseeable catches in your new life you may encounter.

Smart Questions

So you're serious about moving to a small town, but you still have some reservations regarding the sacrifices you think you'll have to make once you leave the city.

Your concern is justified, but in reality you aren't giving anything up: You'll learn to adjust to a community of people who live with a different set of standards when it comes to their physical environments. Usually, it just requires you to make an extra effort, be active instead of passive, which is easy to do in a city crammed with choices in all areas of life. Rural choices are more limited, but most people would agree they're more fulfilling.

Here are some answers to the questions you inevitably have about small town life:

Q. What do I do for entertainment in a small town?
A. Unless the only thing you like to do is walk around the city at two in the morning or go to nightclubs, you should be able to find plenty to do in a small town. Summer theater is quite popular in small towns. Small town America does not have the Radio City Music Halls or Broadway but there is a tremendous amount of pride in local talent. Many small churches, restaurants, pubs and auditoriums offer performances by local musicians, poets and authors.

You must remember that when you move to a small town you may have to reprogram yourself. Hiking, mountain biking, apple-picking and antiquing may not be a source of entertainment where you are now but in the small town, outdoor activity reigns supreme. You don't have to be athletic to enjoy everything the outdoors has to offer.

Q. What about shopping?
A. You may dream of living in a small town but you still love Neiman Marcus and hardware stores the size of football fields.

You don't have to give up your dream of living in a small town if you will settle for close substitutions. You may not find the latest in Paris fashion, but outlet stores are popping up all over the place, many in small towns located in tourist-oriented areas. In Grafton, I live 30 minutes away from J. Crew, The Gap, Polo, Brooks Brothers, Banana Republic, and many other outlet stores.

If gourmet food is your thing, mail order companies can take care of your more esoteric needs. If you can't find it at a nearby farmstand, butcher shop, or even the supermarket, you can order it.

Q. Will I find any intellectual stimulation?
A. A common misconception about a small town is that everyone who lives there is uneducated and uncivilized.

Nothing could be further from the truth. Certainly you will run across people who do not quite hold the same ideas as your friends in the city, but intellectual activity is quite available in small towns everywhere. From local lecture series to public poetry readings, you will certainly not starve for brain stimulation. You may have to look a little harder for the events that excite you, but eventually you will find something entertaining and informative.

As I mentioned earlier, when you move to a small town you have to alter your way of thinking; information is not handed to you quite as frequently or readily as it is in the city or suburbs.

Q. What about medical care?
A. Another common misconception regarding a small town is that there is a complete lack of adequate health care.

Once again, this belief is quite false. In my small town, I often see members of the volunteer ambulance squad spend their weekends to brush up on CPR and proper rescue techniques. They often stay at the volunteer fire department late into the evening making sure they are ready for anything at any time.

Some small town hospitals may not have the technology of the larger cities but the attention given to patients can be a lot more attentive than what you may be used to.

Fitting In When You Stand Out, Part I

You have probably heard the horror stories of people moving to a small town only to find a group of mean-spirited, crabby, reclusive backwoods people who don't seem overly receptive to outsiders.

While there are people who would rather riddle your mailbox with buckshot than invite you to dinner, most of the stories are exaggerations of events that happened in the 1800s. With this in mind, how can you fit into your new small town life without alienating your neighbors?

The most wonderful quality of people who live in small towns is that they hold a tremendous regard for community loyalty. If you tell your neighbor you would gladly help him reshingle his roof, make sure you follow through with the offer. If you help with a barn-raising in a Polo shirt with dockers and L.L. Bean shoes, they may laugh at you a little and tell you that the yacht club is up the road on the left, but most of the time they will be grateful for your help nevertheless.

Fitting in is quite relative and dependent on where you are going and where you are coming from. If you move from New York City to Northern New England, or from San Francisco to Oregon, people will certainly not want to be told how little there is to do in their small town and how in the city you can do this or get that.

Nothing is more annoying than a stranger who walks into a small town and tells everyone he meets how inadequate their town is. Community pride is something that may be nonexistent in many urban neighborhoods, but it's as popular as ever in most small towns.

The way you dress and talk is also going to affect how warmly you are welcomed. It is usually not a wise decision to wear expensive clothes to casual gatherings. People who live in small towns may ignore you if they sense that you're putting on airs, even though you may not agree.

But face it: some people will simply find you unapproachable if they think that your shirt cost more than their car. However, if you are moving to a trendy, touristy small town, your citywear will probably be fine. City transplants tend to be more willing to dress as they did in the city when they are surrounded by other former urbanites.

Aside from your accent, the way you interact with other members of the community is integral in their willingness to accept you. If you are condescending in any way, even if you don't mean to be, you may find yourself sitting by yourself at the picnic table wondering what you said.

People who have grown up in your small town can be sensitive to outsiders who view them as banjo playing yokels. Different media have perpetuated myths about people who live in small towns and therefore, have caused many of them to bare their teeth at the slightest mention of the word hick or bumpkin. It would be wise to deprogram yourself of any media-induced notions of small town life before you pack up your home in the city.

Your willingness to try new things is also important to whether or not you are accepted into a community. Just as many people abroad will encourage you to try native cuisine and entertainment, people in small towns want you to embrace their community as more than just a pretty place to live.

Remember the "when in Rome" cliché? It still holds true in small towns as well. If a neighbor wants you to accompany him on a trip to the junkyard to find a new steering wheel for a 1974 Plymouth, join him and forget about what your friends in the city would think.

In a small town, a haughty attitude won't get you very far. Your new neighbors don't much care what outsiders or the media think of the way they spend their time.

Square dancing and bingo may be sources of jokes for urban America, yet many people living in small towns genuinely enjoy spending a night in a dusty barn line dancing and square dancing as well as screaming BINGO when Minister Joe calls N-34.

Sometimes fitting in can be an awfully difficult task. You'll want to hold onto your own thoughts and beliefs while becoming part of a new community.

The balance can be difficult, trying to avoid conformity while desiring to be accepted by the natives. Through open-mindedness and honesty, the mix can be achieved, along with a bit of patience.

Fitting In When You Stand Out, Part II

People who have never lived in a small town before frequently worry about how to deal with the problems they'll face because they're different in some way from the people who are already there. This may include being Jewish, Asian, single, from California, or whatever. What follows is my admittedly biased opinion about what I've found.

Most often, people in a small town don't care about what you look like or who you sleep with as long as you are sincere about wanting to make a positive contribution to their community.

That said, I must add that this is my perspective

from living in small towns in northern New England for more than a decade. Here, the locals are so used to having people with different beliefs and lifestyles move into their towns that it doesn't much bother them.

I sense that this acceptance via proving yourself may be unique to northern small town areas, but then again, I haven't spent a lot of time in small towns outside of New England, so I don't know if things are different in other parts of the country.

In truth, I know a lot of people in my area who could be considered "different" and who would be shunned by their neighbors in the suburbs or city because of it. Up here, locals may slap a label on you in the beginning if you're "different" in some way, but most will give themselves a chance to know you in the course of everyday life—remember, these towns can be *very* small—and once they do you won't stand out in their eyes.

With that said, in the beginning you're going to stand out. The secret to making it as painless as possible—and remember, you may be so self-conscious about it that you are more aware of your "differences" than anyone else in town—is to blend into the town through your actions.

Here are some suggestions:

- Find someone in town who was once a newcomer, and ask him what he did to fit in. He might say he did nothing; time is often your best friend. Once you make your presence known in the town by regularly visiting the post office and smiling and making eye contact and small talk with the people you run into there, you'll start to distinguish yourself in their eyes. After a few months, they may invite you to drop by for coffee or give you a call to tell you about the upcoming meeting of the garden club.

- Become involved, but not *too* involved from the beginning. In my town, I've found that the small groups that meet once a month or so to talk about and share their crafts ideas, or gab about gardening or even the once-a-month Saturday Women's Brunch at Town Hall always welcome of newcomers. But I wouldn't recommend you start your own group in the first year of living in a new place. Instead, find another person in town who shares your interest in a hobby or activity, and get together regularly to talk about it. Small town life can be very isolating, especially in the long winters up north, and so making an effort to socialize with others in town can win you brownie points.

- This is a two-part suggestion: try to lower your voice. The corollary: keep your mouth shut and your ears open. In the city, you must often raise your voice so that you're heard at all above the racket. In a small town, sometimes even voices at normal volume stand out. The general consensus around here is that if a newcomer moves in and talks loudly all the time, especially at public meetings, he's obviously trying to prove that he's better than us local yokels, especially if he starts to bring up the number of degrees he has or the big Fortune 500 companies where she's worked before. *I* know that you're saying these things because you're probably very nervous about wanting to make a good first impression, but keep in mind that most of the people who live in small towns are probably not going to be impressed by the things that turned your colleagues on in the city. When I first moved to a small town, I trained myself out of my New York accent. Not everyone does this or even wants to, but I felt that this was an important way for me to fit in. You may just choose to lower your voice if you're accustomed to speaking loudly, but whatever you choose, remember that more than what you wear or what you look like, people will evaluate you by what comes out of your mouth.

• Find other newcomers and hang out with them. Through them, you'll start to meet other people in town if they've already made connections. The interesting thing that has happened is that a few of the newcomers to Grafton have sought me out in the last couple of years, which is quite a turn in events. Our non-native status gives us some common ground, as does our work, since an increasing number of newcomers in town work from home.

The trick is to not emphasize your differences; instead, show how much you appreciate the town you've selected by contributing in some way. Because our society puts such an emphasis on the labels we can all put on ourselves, it makes it easier to view the world, but it also creates lots of stress and bitterness. So just start talking to people.

However, there's another aspect of fitting in which I know many people are concerned with, and that is when the difference involves religion, race, and/or politics. I've had some people ask what to do about moving into a town where they're the only Jewish people, or about a mixed-race couple who moves into a small New England town.

Your concerns are justified, to some extent. There are always going to be those people in a small town who are opposed to all newcomers, not just those who are different from them in some way. The sooner you accept this, the better. However, it's been my experience that people in small towns are more accepting of different people because every town has had its local eccentrics, and so are used to congregating with people who differ from the status quo, whatever that is.

Regardless of your difference, fitting in will take time, sometimes years. In the beginning, take it slow, don't call attention to your differences, and act cordial and interested in local goings-on. After all, it took me, a single city woman, a number of years before I felt I was truly accepted in my town.

Chapter Six
Settling In

Congratulations! You've made the move to a small town and are about to start to experience the ways in which your life will change. This will include the way you interact with your new neighbors, establishing a ritualistic afternoon time-out at the general store, or in the case of a popular activity in Grafton, making a mad dash down to the post office at 3:45 each day to make sure your letters and parcels make it on the outgoing mail truck.

Now that you've actually moved, of course you wonder why you made such a big deal about the move. But it's time to get down to business and find out just what being a small-town resident is all about.

My First Month in a Small Town: Derek Scheips

On my first day as a Vermonter, I almost wiped out. *Almost* wiped out is not to be confused with *totally* wiped out, which was how I usually felt before I made the best decision of my life—to leave Manhattan for a small town in Vermont.

Like most New Yorkers, I wasn't used to driving much. On my first day as a Vermonter, I was bopping down a country road in my rental car. Even though I didn't yet have a job, furniture, or money in the bank, I was still pretty pleased with myself. I specialize in ambivalence, but I'd just done something uncharacteristically definitive, had just made a life-changing decision.

A number of cars had been tailgating and passing me on this road. No doubt they thought me a typical tourist, forgetting the gas pedal, my mind lost in the winter scenery. Well, I was not a typical tourist. I had, in fact, just decided to leave my city life behind by signing for an apartment in central Vermont.

The new apartment would do for the moment, I thought. But what would be even nicer was a big farmhouse I saw, set off from the road I was traveling, the one framed with fences and cows, pigs and snow-dusted evergreens, with a big sun hovering over the field behind it. I wanted a closer look. Little did I know my wish was about to come true. A big bearded guy in a red pickup was my latest tailgater. When I decided I'd annoyed this especially big neighbor long enough, I pointed the car into the turnaround in front of this idyllic farm.

I soon found out it wasn't really a turnaround. I basically ran my car off the road. I rocked and bumped down an embankment, finally settling on a patch of powder and ice about ten feet from the road. A few inches further and I would have gone down a hill, causing a herd of cows and pigs to stampede from their rustic pen.

After a moment, I got out of the car without injury. The cows and pigs looked at me curiously, and two German shepherd and a beagle tied to the house porch began to hurl a chorus of woofs and yelps in my direction. Peaceful Vermont vistas are what lured me here, but what had I done? I went and ruined one of the prettiest scenes on my very first day. Not the best start on a new life.

Embarrassed, I wanted to get my car out of the people's front yard, and quick. But much to my dismay, the trunk did not contain a shovel. The dogs continued to bark and I kicked at the snow and ice around the wheels. I got back into the car and put it in reverse, but it only moved a few inches. Then I put the gears into forward and got myself even more stuck, the snow now turning brown from my hopeless wheel-spinning. The dogs barked louder.

Then a woman appeared on the porch, a kind-looking fortyish woman in a gray sweatshirt and jeans. She shushed the dogs and strolled toward me and my car.

"I'm so sorry to be disturbing you," I said. "I can't seem to get out."

"Don't worry about it," she said. "It's a beautiful day. I was just about to come outside to do some things anyway."

I explained that I had mistaken the lawn for a turnaround, and she assured me that it happened all the time.

"We don't even mow this part in the summer. The cars take care of the grass."

I tried to reverse again with her directing me from the front of the car. I made a bit of progress toward the road, but kept hitting new patches of ice, and halting. Even with one of us pushing, it wasn't working.

"We need sand," she said. The chastened dogs growled at me as I walked with her to a nearby shed. The shed had a number of hanging shovels as well as sand, and we each grabbed one.

Digging out my car, between my periodic apologies for ruining her peaceful sunny afternoon, we chatted. I learned that her family had owned the farm for several generations. Her name was Patty and she asked me what I was doing up in the area. I told her that I came to look at apartments because I wanted to leave New York. I mentioned some of the towns I had checked out in New Hampshire and Vermont.

"Stay in Vermont," Patty said.

I told her I'd actually just signed for an apartment in Vermont in the next town.

"You made the right choice," she said, without further explanation.

Thus I was introduced to one of the central mysteries of the area: people's loyalties to either Vermont or New Hampshire. As a newcomer in this border area, I thought that the towns in both states were fairly similar; at least many *looked* similar. But I would soon find out that the people who live here, often have definite opinions about which state is better, and why. Since I figured that Patty wasn't going to explain her bias towards Vermont, I decided to let the subject drop.

With the sand and shovel, we got the car backed up about five feet from the road. As luck would have it, two joggers came around the bend, stopped, and provided the extra pushing needed to finally slide my car back onto the road. Soon I was on my merry way.

Compared to my first day, the rest of my first month was uneventful. I returned the rental car, and I needed to be at the apartment to wait for my things to be delivered from the city. Each day I walked a few blocks to the post office and country store, but I didn't meet many of my neighbors coming or going those first weeks.

Without humans around, I turned my attentions to the animal kingdom. My kitchen window looks out onto a lawn with a bird feeder, with an abandoned railroad track and woods as the background. I got my binoculars and watched bluebirds, cardinals, and robins flock to the seeds every day. Drama came in the form of a small black kitten that started to stalk, not very successfully, the birds and squirrels in my back yard. With my binoculars I had spotted an owl a few times in a nearby tree, and I was haunted by the idea that this owl would snatch up the kitten like one of those flying monkeys in *The Wizard of Oz*. But so far, the kitten has survived.

Clearly, after years of living at a big city pace, I suddenly had too much time on my hands. But during my first month in a small town, I was happy to discover one of my previously untapped talents—doing nothing. Vermont, and probably New Hampshire, are great places to do nothing at all.

Confessions of a Flatlander, a/k/a A Person From Away

The following story was written by Donna Dubuc, an urban transplant who learned to view her city-to-small town transformation in the best light: with humor.

You don't need special detection glasses to spot one of us in a group. We do our best to fit in, but we still stick out. Our long underwear is always brand new. Our duck boots have alligators on them. And we all owned four-wheel drive vehicles six years before moving here. We came from places like Boston, New York, or as in my case, Washington, D.C.

Like immigrants at Ellis Island, we came looking for a better life. We follow images of roaring fireplaces, horsedrawn sleds, and ATMs without a wait or robbery. After living here a while, though, we realize that small town living requires certain adjustments. I miss getting pizza delivered to my door. My real fantasy, however, is seeing a U.S. mail carrier or garbage man swing by once in a while.

You have to be self-reliant up here. I used to take running water and indoor plumbing for granted. In the city, I could get hot or cold water out of one faucet. I couldn't drink the water, but I had an endless supply of it. I'm not even sure I'm qualified to manage my own utilities. To be perfectly honest, I don't understand the difference between a dug and a drilled well. I figure that hard water is what Jesus walked on. And a dry spell is what all my single friends over 35 are going through.

I worry that if the well doesn't go dry, surely I'll overwhelm the septic system. By the way, I was perfectly comfortable parting with my family's waste; I never wanted to keep it in the backyard. Leach fields are never pictured on post cards and calendars. They are part of "the unphotographed Vermont" like personal salvage yards filled with abandoned vehicles.

My move to a small town has also forced me to face fears that I should have outgrown. It gets darker at night here. I'm less afraid of walking through a four-level urban parking garage at night than of feeling my way to our detached garage. I'm convinced I'll be the first one to spot a "returned for revenge" catamount as it pounces on me. There's also a black bear out there willing to give up berries and nuts for my cellulite-rich thighs. And everyone knows homicidal maniacs hang out in the woods, looking for houses far from the road so no one can hear their victims scream.

Besides irrational fears, the other major issue I'm tackling is trust. I am suspicious of people who stop for me to cross the street. In the city, a car is not a mode of transportation, it's a weapon. If a car stops for me, I figure it's a disgruntled postal worker who needs to reload. As a pedestrian, I'm as vulnerable as a lame deer in November.

It's hard to let go of urban paranoia. No matter how hard I try not to. I still like locks; they make me feel safe. I can't leave a bicycle outside a store without a kryptonite padlock that Superman couldn't pick without the help of a 13-year-old gang member. I take my purse with me for communion. I won't leave my car running while I dart into a convenience store unless it has three uniformed marines in it. The cat has to use a secret knock to get back into the house.

Despite all these transitions, I am certain that moving to a small town has been good for me. Spring is here so I can stop worrying about needing another cord of wood. Runoff water should replenish my well. And once the weather warms up, I think I'll try sleeping with the windows open without my brass knuckles.

The Little Things to Expect When You Move to a Small Town

Occasionally, I'm accused of trying too hard to convince people that they *shouldn't* move to a small town, or at least of bursting their long-running fantasies so that they're not caught off guard when they do relocate to a small town area.

So here are some tips about the benefits of small town life. Here are some of the positive ways my life changed when I moved to a small town, and the good things you can expect from your future life there.

- People look you in the eye, which makes everything seem a little bit more personal. Eye contact is extinct in big cities. Get used to it in a small town. It took me awhile.

- You'll feel like you're part of a community; happily, this can happen exceedingly fast to a newcomer. The first time you drive down the road and the guy you spoke to for ten seconds at the general store the other day waves to you, you'll feel as though you belong there.

- Your blood pressure and medical bills will go down. When you don't have to deal with traffic jams, endless noise and masses of humanity, your body will naturally relax.

- Your overall expenses will go down, which eliminates much of the temptation to buy something every time you leave the house. The mall is not a block away. The urban status patterns of wanting to live better than your neighbors is pretty much nonexistent in a small town; if you do decide to subscribe to it, you'll probably find that no one around you will care and may even ostracize you.

- Life will feel more manageable. Yes, your job may revolve around a project on a global scale, but in a small town your immediate world is boiled down to your family, your job, and your community. Being a big fish doesn't matter here, but many people find that it's easier to become involved with local issues—or join a few clubs—because the scale is so much smaller and easier to deal with.

- You can be a hermit if you want...or you'll at least be able to easily choose the people who come across your path. The Jehovah's Witnesses may head up your driveway at least once a month, but these common experiences make for great stories to share with your neighbors.

- If all or most of these aspects of small town life are what you're looking for, then the number one benefit you'll reap from living in a small town is that you'll be happier.

People Over 50 in a Small Town

For people over 50—or those who are fast approaching it—moving to a small town may require more than a majestic view and a pretty house. Proximity to a hospital and supermarket, road conditions, and the existence of an active community of mature people are all primary concerns to the over-50 person who wants to relocate to a small town.

Medical attention will usually be first and foremost on your mind as you prepare to leave the city or suburbs. Perhaps you need the comfort and ease that comes with living within a couple of blocks of a major hospital. If this is the case, your next step is easy. Call the chamber of commerce in the area you wish to move to and get a listing of all of the hospitals in the area. Follow this up with a phone call to a real estate agent and explain exactly what you're looking for. For other people, however, the mere fact that their house is easily accessible by emergency crews is enough.

The next task is equally simple and will provide you with more leeway in deciding where you want to live. Drive through a typical small town and locate a house that seems to have everything you want, from

the setting, style, and location. Call the fire department in the town and explain that you're concerned
about the length of time it would take an ambulance to
make it to the property.

With the new 911 laws—i.e., in New Hampshire,
all residences are linked to a central 911 service—that
tells emergency dispatchers the exact location of your
house if you are unable to communicate it to them—
gone are the days of explaining where on Tucker
Mountain you live, for example, past the old Johnson
Farm but before Gooseneck Pond.

As I have mentioned, the EMT squads in small
towns that I have witnessed show a sincere dedication
to providing excellent care for their neighbors. And
because they are your neighbors, chances are that their
response time may be measured in seconds, not minutes.

Before you start your phone calls, however, you
should think about what your road is going to look like
in the winter. If you are planning a move to a warmer
climate, you can disregard this advice. However, if you
have your heart set on the north country, read on.
Seemingly wonderful roads can quickly become skating rinks when winter rears its head. Ask some of your
potential neighbors what the road is like in winter and
in spring—a/k/a mud season—and then take them
seriously.

If they have horror stories to tell about sliding cars
and six-foot snow drifts, you may want to reconsider
your move if you think that severe and lengthy winter
weather will bother you. However, you're more likely
to hear different tales about how the road is very
well-plowed and maintained in winter.

Depending on your health and how well you get
around, you may also want to consider proximity to a
grocery store to be on your list of priorities. I live

twenty minutes from the nearest supermarket, and believe me when I say that twenty minutes becomes an hour when it's snowing; in the sweltering heat of summer, without an air conditioner in your car, the trip seems just as long.

At the very least, you may want to make sure you are close to a mini-mart or small town general store so you can purchase staple items when necessary. If there is something you often need that your small town store doesn't carry, ask the shopkeeper to order it for you; more often than not, she will be glad to, though it may take a few days to arrive.

After these initial considerations, the list can become pretty specific: some people may wish to be close to a pharmacy, others want to be near a park, while others simply need to be near a lake with a good supply of freshwater bass.

The best advice is to sit down and make a list of the things you desire, right down to the last detail, and find the closest thing to perfect that you can. But keep in mind, of course, that no place will have everything on your wish list.

Another concern may be the presence of an active community of people your age. Whether you're looking for a local senior center or club, or just the assurance that there are other people around who will make you feel like you're part of the town, the best place to start, once again, is the chamber of commerce.

Ask for a listing of all of the senior organizations in the surrounding towns and their phone numbers. Once the list arrives, start making phone calls to get more detailed information and ask to be put on the mailing list. If you can, try to attend a few events before you move. This will make you familiar to them so that when you do make the move, you will already be part of the gang.

Caretaking 101

Despite the fact that you're educating yourself about the ways in which a small town move would affect your life, you may still be hesitant about making the move; after all, it will be a major change in your life.

A great way to "try before you buy," so to speak, is to become the caretaker of a property in a small town. Gary Dunn, the editor of *Caretaker's Gazette*, provides the basics here. He's also included a couple of profiles of people who have become caretakers so you can hear from a few people who left their conventional lifestyles to follow their dreams of small town living without the hassles and headaches of wondering how they were going to pay the bills. And the good news is that there are loads of caretaking jobs out there; for one, Gary's newsletter lists jobs all over the world.

Q: What is a caretaker?
A: For those who are not involved in the profession, the word "caretaker" may have numerous meanings. But for the growing number of people who are dedicated to the caretaking profession and land stewardship, a caretaker is a property caretaker: a person hired by a landowner to care for his property in exchange for compensation.

Q: What is land stewardship?
A: Land stewardship is the concept of caring for land to ensure that it remains intact and productive for future generations. Caretakers act as land stewards when their responsibilities include preservation and maintenance activities. To quote Wendell Berry, author of *The Unsettling of America*, "The care of the earth is our most ancient and most worthy, and after all, our

most pleasing responsibility. To cherish what remains of it, and to foster its renewal, is our only legitimate hope."

Q: Is caretaking a new profession?
A: No, it's actually a very old profession, rooted in the British tradition of land maintenance. In 1868 the *Times of London* defined a caretaker as "a person put in charge of a farm from which the tenant has been evicted." Today, that definition has been expanded to cover a multitude of landowner/caretaker relationships. The number and diversity of these relationships has increased during the past decade. As more and more landowners hire caretakers to watch over their property, the caretaking profession continues to grow in popularity.

Q: Who hires caretakers?
A: Many different types of property owners hire caretakers. Landowners, large and small, individuals or institutions, can benefit by utilizing the services of a qualified caretaker. Farmers, ranchers, homesteaders, estates, camps, parks, lodges, and nature preserves all employ caretakers.

Q: What skills and experience are required for caretaking?
A: While many landowners seek experienced caretakers with specific skills (e.g. maintenance, farming, ranching or animal husbandry) others are willing to take on and train people with general backgrounds. As with most other occupations, such traits as honesty, common sense, and flexibility are key prerequisites. For caretakers who live and work alone on the property of an absentee landowner, the ability to function independently and fulfill one's responsibilities without

daily guidance and instruction from the landowner are important qualifications. Although a love of nature and solitude is important, having hobbies and interests (e.g. reading, writing, painting, photography) that can be pursued in what are often remote areas is extremely helpful.

Q: What are the responsibilities of a caretaker?
A: The duties and responsibilities of a caretaker are as varied as the landowners and caretakers themselves. Caretaking can give one the opportunity to work in dozens of areas: groundskeeping, land stewardship, farming, organic gardening, forestry, ranching, animal husbandry and fisheries. While some landowners just require a presence on their property, others need fences mended, snow plowed, gardens tended, animals cared for, and houses, roads and pastures maintained. Plumbing and electrical work may be part of a caretaker's duties, or the caretaker may be responsible for hiring competent repairmen.

Q: What should one consider when applying for a caretaking position?
A: The prudent caretaker sets out to develop a working relationship with the landowner, his or her prospective employer. If the landowner's goals and philosophies are stated in their advertisement, prospective caretakers should consider whether these are in harmony with their own beliefs. While skill and experience are important, most landowners are initially concerned with character references. When answering an ad, a neatly prepared resume should be accompanied by photographs of oneself (and family, if applicable) and references. Landowners often request a personal letter, where the prospective care-

taker discusses such things as interests, goals and reasons for desiring a caretaking position. It is helpful to be as open and honest as possible. Information regarding any special skills or interests should also be included.

Q: Is caretaking suitable for retirees?
A: Yes. In fact, many landowners specifically request "mature" or "retired" individuals or couples when placing their ads. Retirees bring with them a wealth of skills and experience that can be readily used when caretaking property. Landowners like the fact that many retirees have a second income. In exchange for caretaking responsibilities retirees are able to live rent-free and experience life in different geographic areas.

Q: Are there any financial benefits for landowners who hire caretakers?
A: Putting their property in the hands of a qualified caretaker can free landowners from the responsibility of day-to-day maintenance. This arrangement can enable them to increase their profits in the long run. A caretaker who lives on the property ensures that it is kept in good condition, secure from vandalism, theft and maintenance problems. He or she also makes any necessary improvements or repairs so that the property always remains in top condition. Having a qualified caretaker on one's property gives the landowner time to pursue other interests or employment.

Q: Can caretaking provide any special opportunities for travelers?
A: Inveterate travelers have discovered that caretak-

ing enables them to live and work in a variety of interesting locales—both in the U.S. and abroad. Positions may be for the long or short-term, seasonal or year-round. Many newcomers to the caretaking field have been lifelong travelers. Most are motivated by the desire to live a simple, small town life or explore another culture in depth. Caretaking offers travelers the opportunity to become a part of a community and experience life as the locals live it. Travelers can caretake resort properties during off-seasons, enjoying the use of the facilities. For travelers who are considering a move to another area, caretaking allows them to experience life in a new location prior to spending time, money and energy relocating there.

Q: Can full or part-time RVers find employment as caretakers?

A: Yes. Many RVers are discovering that caretaking is a challenging and fulfilling occupation. It enables them to take some time off the road, settle down for a period of time, and enjoy life in another location. It's an economical way to live as site and utility hookups are provided by the landowner. RVers are often in demand by landowners whose properties do not have separate housing for caretakers; RVers require only hookups. While some campgrounds that hire RVers as caretakers require light duties, others are simply in need of "site-sitters." In both situations, there is plenty of leisure time to enjoy the property and its amenities. RVers can also find employment as caretakers on properties of landowners who travel. In this instance, it is important to maintain the property and make it appear occupied. Seasonal or short-term positions permit RVers to maintain their freewheeling lifestyle.

Caretakers Sandra and Deane Maxson

The Maxsons are a couple perfectly suited to each other and the lush semitropical ranch they caretake in southwest Florida. They are year-round employees on a 90,000-acre ranch which is the site of a cattle operation, farming, mining and hunting. There is a large hunting lodge, snuggled away in the midst of a forest of Telegraph Cypress on an island. Deane maintains each and every campsite throughout the year. He also takes care of the hunting blinds plus the mechanical feeders which have timers and batteries. The mechanical feeders are suspended from trees and need to be filled and checked every week.

Sandra plans and organizes a number of elaborate events for her employer. Sandra does a lot of canning while Deane keeps up with the maintenance of the lodge and the citrus grove. This entails mowing the grounds, fertilizing, painting the decks, porches, railings, and outside redwood furniture. Their compensation includes a salary of $2,000 per month, housing, medical insurance, a two week unpaid vacation in the summer months, and a gratuity check in late spring after hunting season. The gratuity is based on the number of hunting parties that visited during that season.

For their next caretaking position, the Maxsons are willing to relocate. They're interested in managing a bed and breakfast inn, a dude ranch, or even a farm or ranch. They don't smoke or use drugs themselves but have no objection to others who smoke or drink. Sandra and Deane are lucky—they're healthy, happy, and have found the right environment and occupation to enjoy life.

Caretaker Mike Peterson

Mike Peterson is a very versatile guy. After growing up on a farm in Wisconsin, spending some time in college, doing a Navy hitch, and getting married, he set off on the railroad to become a locomotive engineer. After 12 years on the railroad, and a divorce, he traveled the "lower 48" for several years then settled in Alaska. He's been there for seven years. For the past five years, Mike has been the winter caretaker at Valhalla Lodge, located on a remote lake in western Alaska. Valhalla Lodge is one of Alaska's premiere fishing and hunting lodges. It was built for those who truly appreciate the great outdoors. People from all over the world make the trip to experience a real wilderness paradise. The only access to the lodge is by plane, using either floats in the summer or skis when the lake is frozen. Once Mike arrives at Valhalla Lodge, he's alone for the next seven months, except for Bandit, the company dog. His duties are to "be there," and make sure the lodge and all its belongings are still there when the fishing season starts the next spring. If something breaks, he fixes it. When it snows, he cleans the wings of the four planes parked there. Other than that, Mike may do nothing for long periods of time.

He's paid $300 per month, plus a $1,000 bonus at the end of the season. Mike says "that's OK for a single guy with no bills." The two most common questions people ask Mike are, "Have you seen the movie, *The Shining*?" (which he has several times) and, "How can you stand to be out there all by yourself for so long?"

His reply to that question is, "How can you stand to go out every morning in the dark, in the cold, shovel off your car, hope it starts, so you can play 'bumper cars' to get to a job you probably do not like, where you don't make enough money, so you can pay rent on a place you're probably not crazy about anyway?" On mornings like that, Mike just makes another pot of coffee, puts his feet up on the table, and watches all of Good Morning America on RAT-NET (Small town Alaska Television Network). As he sits at his table watching it get light outside, he can observe a line of caribou crossing the ice, or a couple of moose walking along the lake's shore. It's things like this that make the long winters worthwhile for Mike.

Copyright *The Caretaker Gazette*. Published since 1983, the Gazette is a bimonthly newsletter that helps landowners and caretakers find one another. The Caretaker Gazette, Gary C. Dunn, Publisher, PO Box 5887, Carefree, AZ 85377-5887 USA (602) 488-1970; caretaker@uswest.net; http://www.angelfire.com/wa/caretaker

Chapter Seven
Your New Life in a Small Town

Once you begin to spend any amount of time as the resident of a small town, certain truths will quickly come to reveal themselves. One, is the pecking order of certain individuals in town, usually those who are just louder than others. The second is more mundane, but probably more surprising: people in a small town live their lives the same way you do and share many of the same concerns. Plus, they're probably as busy as you were when you were living in the city.

This is a surprise because for many people who yearn for small-town life, once they finally make it there and discover that their new neighbors are as connected to and interested in the world as any city person, it may be somewhat of a letdown. It may help to keep things in perspective: whenever you've visited a small town in the past, it's probably been on vacation, where your mindset necessarily colors the philosophies of the people who live there. Now that you're living there, too, and working every day, you may be dismayed to find your energy and attitude towards your work may be too city-like for you. "Wait a minute, I thought moving to a small town was supposed to help me to relax!"

It will, and it does. You just need some time to

adjust.

How Will The Locals Treat You?

People occasionally ask me how I think natives and locals will treat them once they move to their small town nirvana. I tell them not to look at the locals but at themselves first. Awhile back, I got a call from a guy who had moved from Long Island to a small town in Pennsylvania, and in a loud, coarse voice he proceeded to tell me how the people in his new area shunned him from the start.

"If you ever want to do a story on the negative parts of small town living, you should give me a call," he informed me. "I'm an expert."

It wasn't too difficult to see why his new neighbors were so turned off; he probably inflicted his opinions on them in the same manner that he was delivering them to me—his voice boomed so much that I had to hold the phone away from my ear as he was delivering his diatribe.

I don't mean to single this type out, because I've found that the overwhelming majority of people who make the move to a small town are pleasant and willing to make concessions to their neighbors, and able to accept the myriad, often unpredictable inconveniences that go along with small town life.

But whenever I hear people from away comment if only they could move here their lives would be perfect, I wonder.

Out west, there's been a veritable war going on between locals and newcomers for almost a decade now. A friend of mine who moved from New York to Missoula, Montana in 1992 was recently quoted in *USA*

Today on the subject of newcomers:

"They think they are moving to a movie," she said. "Montana is not a movie. It's cold, there are no jobs, and people are suspicious of transients. I get calls all the time from strangers who say, 'I just moved here. I came for vacation for a week and I loved it so I left my job and my friends, and by the way I'm looking for work. Do you have any ideas?' And I'm thinking to myself, 'This person is a moron!' What I tell them is that this is a 19th-century agrarian culture. Come because you love what it is. If you like where you left, stay there."

After reading my cautions about small-town life, one woman told me that she likes what I have to say, but she sometimes feels as if I am paid by a conspiracy of small town residents who have a vested interest in keeping newcomers out. I know that I go overboard at times, but in a way I feel that I have to lean too far in this direction in order to repair the damage inflicted by the magazines, tourism councils, and economic development boards that I think paint small town life in too rosy a fashion.

After all, there are tens of thousands of people who drop everything and move to a small town not because they've carefully done their homework about what to expect as you are, but because spending your days canning or raising sheep sounds like fun, or because an airbrushed photograph of a perfect sunset makes them want to drop everything and escape smoggy sunsets.

I love living in a small town. I live the kind of life I want to here, and I feel very fortunate that I am able to live and work in a place I love. But I also know that my lifestyle is rare, and that most people who move to a small town will have to bring along some stresses and frustrations that they thought would be magically left behind in the city. Moving to a small town is like losing the last ten pounds: it's not a panacea.

As trend soothsayer Faith Popcorn correctly predicted a few years ago, escapism has fast taken root in American society, and one of the most popular methods is to move to a small town. But you should be very clear about your reasons as well as accepting the fact that you'll have to do some changing.

Staying Happy Once You Make It to a Small Town

You're perfectly capable of leaving behind your unsatisfying city life for a brighter future living in a small town. However, you may be so determined to move that you don't have a clue what to do to remain content once the last box has been unpacked. Some people who have moved from the city to a small town are quite surprised to discover they may feel a sense of isolation so strong they start to wish for the dirty city streets they thought they had left behind forever. Others discover after the fact that they really don't like living in the woods after all. There is no secret to remaining happy once you get there. What it does take is time and understanding.

You may simply want to live the hermit's life and have nothing to do with anyone or anything. If that is the life you want, you will surely get it but be prepared for the effects. Exclusion from a community means exclusion from assistance when your pipes freeze or you barn needs reshingling.

When you first feel the symptoms of dissatisfaction with the small town life you have chosen, try to remember what it was that created your desire to relocate to begin with. If it was the image the media created, you certainly have problems; but if you escaped the city because you wanted a better life for you and your family, then look at all you've got.

Many urbanites suffer from the Grass is Greener Syndrome once they arrive in a small town. When they were living in the city, they would look at the smog and filth and dream of clean small town living. However, after a few months in a small town they began dreaming of real bagels and nightlife. This may not happen to you but if it does, confront it. Immerse yourself in small town activities and give it some time. Visit the city to binge on the things you left behind. Hopefully the feelings will subside and you'll feel confident that your move was the right one. If not, maybe a small town was never your style, and you should cut your losses.

This brings me to the point of etiquette when involving yourself in community activities. So often I have seen ordinary, nice people from the city join a school board or town planning board and become power-brokers in sheep's clothing. I recall one teacher from the city joining the staff of a small-town elementary school and attempting to change the way children had been taught for decades. The fact that this particular teacher wanted to change the school was truly valiant, for she was bringing a unique outlook to a school that was stuck in old ways. The problem occurred because the teacher alienated everyone, parents and teachers, by insisting that her way was the only way.

Staying happy in a small town is dependent only on you. But be wise as you get your feet wet in the community. Do not trample on old beliefs, but suggest alternatives, and back down when you sense it's time. After all, a big part of your happiness will depend on whether you feel at home in your new town and how the community accepts you.

Why Did You Pick Your Small Town? One Man's Story

Larry Hall, 55, is a consultant who has lived in Chicago since 1969. But he and his wife have begun plans to move to a town in Michigan called Northport, with a population of 400 year-round. Northport is on a peninsula that is bounded on one side by Lake Michigan and on the other by Grand Traverse Bay. It's approximately 360 miles from Chicago, and Hall and his wife built a house on the Bay ten years ago. They plan to move there full-time in a couple of years, and they now visit it on weekends about once a month in the winter and for some longer visits in summer.

Since it's always helpful to know why some people have picked a particular small town place to live, here's what Larry said:

"We settled on Northport because most of the people I know in Chicago who have second houses have them in areas where most of the weekend and summer residents are also people from Chicago, either the southern end of Lake Michigan or Lake Geneva in Wisconsin. I really wanted to have a house in a place where I was not hanging out with the same kind of people I hang out with in Chicago. I wanted people who were interested in different things, focused on different interests, and had different lives from my friends in Chicago. Northport has wonderful people who have different interests and who live at a different pace. That was a large part of it.

"We also wanted to be in a small town area and have proximity to a body of water. I did spend some time in a house in southern Michigan, and it was like a progressive dinner in Chicago: I would see the same people there that I would see back in Chicago, except I had to drive an hour to see them in their summer houses.

"I'm ready to leave because a lot of the patterns of how I live today are determined by the fact that I live in a large city: the intensity in which I approach work, the lifestyle that I've created, the things I spend money and time on. Everyone I know is focused on exactly the same things, and I would like to know more about the kinds of interests I would pursue if I didn't have the stimulus of the city. I believe I would find interests that I don't have, and I believe I would find things that are much more important to me than I realize because I don't have access to them now. I would like to experience all of that.

"Another reason is I would like to do more writing, and I believe that to do that, I would need to reduce my exposure to the work that I do right now so that I open up space for writing. I find that when I'm out at the house in Northport, I allow myself much more time for reflection and for a certain amount of passiveness, which I don't allow myself in the city.

"To prepare for our move we're working on scaling back our cash flow needs. We're reducing our debt and increasing saving in retirement funds. I'm also beginning to do some writing as a way to create a passive income stream. It's not the kind of thing you can start once you're there; I have to have it already on line.

"But I do fear some things about the move, mainly missing my friends and finding out that I'm going to miss things that are available to me in Chicago much more than I anticipate now. I don't even know that I will miss them until I miss them.

"But this is what I won't miss: Now, I spend a lot of time being alert to the potential dangers around me, whether it's the number of drivers on the road, or the crime statistics for my neighborhood, or the news I see every night on TV. I pay a lot of attention to protecting myself and my family from danger. I want to see what it would feel like to be free of that."

Does Small Town Living = Being Anti-Social?

Awhile back, I posted the following note on one of the rural newsgroups on the Internet:

"One thing I notice in some posts is how much people who live in the boonies—and those who want to—hate the idea of having other people around, or in their face. You don't want to share a driveway, see another house, or hear the road.

"I know I belong to this group. I have a loooooooong driveway, I can't hear any traffic, and you can't see any houses that are closer than five miles away. I work at home, sometimes don't go out for a couple of days, and go to the supermarket either at 11 at night or early in the morning. (It's 40 minutes away)

"I have 12 acres and enough space to do what I want to. I wasn't always like this, but I've found that most of my human contact comes when I wave to my neighbors when they drive by, or I chat with them for a few minutes in the general store, I just prefer not being around people too much.

"Any thoughts? Similar experiences?"

The responses were fascinating:

"My experience is similar. Actually I'm very gregarious, have many close longtime friends, and like meeting new people all the time—but I want real privacy when I'm home. In part it's because I play piano many hours daily and don't want to be heard (nor disturb others). But it's more basic. I just want the privacy.

"In part, it's because I found the American levels of presumed intrusiveness so extremely high, especially with noise. People make increasingly bizarre assumptions that the noise they make—mostly from consumer toys from TV and radio to motorcycle and leafblower, also dog barking—can rightfully enter others' homes. I love quiet.

"Often when I pass a nice neighborhood, or even a nice apartment building, I think how nice it could be to live with other people around. But only if they were quiet and polite (and I played piano elsewhere).

"Solitude is ineffably wonderful. A treasure oasis, sanctuary, inspiration. I'm a writer as well as a pianist, and need solitude for practical purposes of work as much as I love it for ethereal purposes of life."

—*Kenneth L., Nova Scotia*

"No, I don't call this anti-social. I love people, but my best dream is to be able to sit on my porch for up to two hours at a time without hearing *one* sound made any a nonnatural source. That includes truck/car sounds, voices, shots, stereos, blasting, drilling, *nothing*! Just a nice little plot of my woods on one side, a dry creek on another, and a dirt road for the mailman to drive on. Close to perfect."

—David L., Texas

"Have you by any chance seen the movie *Barfly?* Your remarks remind me of the main character Henry Chinanski. When asked if he hated people he responded, 'No, but I feel better when they're not around.'

"I don't think people out in a small town areas are anti-social, often they are just too damn busy to socialize. When neighbors do drop by, we set things aside and really get down to visiting. Same with the church socials and community events. When these occur, people attend and have a really good time. When one doesn't have much time for jawin', they really enjoy it when they do get the time."

"I don't consider myself anti-social because I live in a small town and value my solitude. Among other things I value also the intellectual, cultural, and social contacts that my 40- and 70-mile proximity to two major cities allows. I realize I would not be happy without these contacts. Still, I find the nighttime cries of coyote packs roaming the surrounding prairie strangely comforting in marked contrast to the roar of freeway traffic and the other noise commonly heard in the city."

—Harold A., Texas

"I don't think it's anti-social. I think of anti-socialness as being actively against society. Most of the small town people I know (and I grew up in a small town area) are not rude. They may be standoffish to people they don't know, but not 'anti-social.' I think the attitude you are talking about is more of a 'non-socialness,' the desire to do without socializing most of the time.

"I also find this attitude is somewhat more common in people who are not living near where they grew up. I find that the social bonds many small town people rely on take a lifetime to form. This is not always the case though. I know one lady who lived in the suburbs most of her life. Within a year or so of moving to the backside of the boonies, she said that she knew her neighbors (those within five miles) better than she had ever gotten to know those within five houses from her old home. Me? I'm planning on moving back to a small town area in part because I hope it will improve my socializing; I never did get 'city-people' figured out. :-)"

—*Paul H.*

"I have a similar setting: no neighbors in sight, the house is at the end of a two-mile driveway. The only downside is that I sometimes have wildlife gawkers and tourists, but my feeling in this regard is quite European: as long as they respect the land, leave it as they found it and do not inhibit farming, then they are welcome. Hunters are an exception. They must register or they will be arrested for trespassing; I had a bad experience two years ago when a shotgun slug hit the house near the side door.)

"One particularly interesting point is that while there are only a dozen or so residences within several miles and we rarely visit, we do know of each other and nobody is alone when there is a crisis or living becomes difficult.

"I could telecommute, but I'm still a people-person and feel compelled to come to town almost every day."

—*John S.*

"We have six acres with a little travel trailer in the foothills of the Sierra. We retreat there from L.A. every two or three weeks (wish it could be the other way around). It is so crowded in the city I feel I can't even think; there is such an overload of information--much of it useless, but you have to sift through it--and lots of people who want to waste your time. My husband thinks I'm anti-social, but I disagree. I'm just trying to defend myself from all this overload. If a friend or even a relative stranger is in need, I help. In a small town, when I've had my time to think, stroll my property and appreciate what new flowers have come up, what new birds are passing through, etc., then I enjoy chatting with neighbors."

—*Cheryl Q., California*

"I think it does make people anti-social. When people are in the habit of encountering others, they get in the habit of doing so. When people are in the habit of being alone, they adjust to it.

"I have hundreds of students around me every day and at night I retire to my 1000 acres. And I get annoyed when someone comes down the drive to *my* home. I see the same in my neighbors: one runs a computer company during the week while others just farm.

"In cities you have no choice, or little choice; in a small town you do. The people in a small town are there because they like the things there are to do in a small town. The thought of a crowded bar, loud noise, people talking about basketball or their kids or their new dress makes me welcome the fact that my hen is due to hatch her chicks soon, the pines need pruning, and the new foal needs worming."

—*Arnold C., New Zealand*

Troubleshooting

Kathy Babbitt is author of the book *Downscaling* (Moody Press, 1993), with her husband, David. They also published a newsletter on the subject, *Downscaling 46510*, which they recently sold.

When they moved to tiny Claypool, Indiana, population 750 and an hour away from Fort Wayne, in 1990, they were fulfilling a lifelong dream and thought they would live there for the rest of their lives. Now, as soon as David can find another job as a private pilot, they'll sell their house and move back to a more populated area.

Why didn't the Babbitts' dream work out? And what can you learn from their experience? Here's what Kathy has to say on where they are now and what's next.

Q: Why did you move to Claypool?

A: Dave is a private pilot, and over the course of two years, he had been gone for a total of 480 days. We had also moved a total of 45 times—from Alaska to Africa—since we were married. In order to leave, he would had to go on unemployment before he could find another job. So he didn't sign his renewal contract. We chose the midwest for its lower cost of living, and we liked the change of seasons. We also had just come from living in Texas for three years. And I'd always wanted to live on a lake; our house is like our own state park out in the middle of nowhere.

Q: When did things first start to go wrong for you?

A: We have a beautiful location. It was great in the beginning to unwind from the hectic pace, but you can only unwind for so long. Then you have to have something brought back into your life to make it challenging and rewarding again.

For me, the major problem came when my kids got older and I had no purpose for staying home. My role changed: my world no longer revolved around me and my kids. I also had expected more community involvement than what we've had. I guess I could have made more of an effort to get involved, but the desire just wasn't there. We've traveled a lot and are more broadminded than a lot of people, and a lot of the challenge was gone. I miss having interaction with people of a like mind-set. Normally, when we moved to a new place, we wanted to meet a lot of new people and get into a new culture and really conquer it. The challenge is gone because we had done it so many times.

We also have a lot of cloud coverage in every season except summer because we're on a lake, and I find that the older I get the more I'm affected by lack of sunshine.

We published the newsletter for two years, and we wrote the book, in addition to my marketing business, so that's kept me occupied. But I haven't found any meaningful opportunities here. Some other professional goals I have will make having to stay longer more palatable.

I've had no problems running my business, since people find out about what I do and then they find me. However, the telecommunications here are antiquated; we can't get call waiting or call forwarding, which makes it more difficult.

Q: What would you have done differently?

A: I would have chosen a different location. It's not the country per se, it's the cold weather and the different culture. You need a certain amount of mental stimulation. I recently traveled to Texas and Chicago and while I was there, I felt, I'm alive again and there are real people here.

Q: Do you find that natives are particularly reticent about getting to know newcomers?

A: Some, but not necessarily. One of the reasons why we haven't become involved is because my husband, who found another job as a private pilot, is on call a lot, and whenever we invited people to dinner, we had to cancel. So I just stopped, and that was the beginning of the breakdown of our social network here: we didn't have a schedule we could count on. If I had made more of an effort to get more involved in the community, I probably wouldn't have felt so isolated.

Q: What's the next place you want to live?
A: I'm looking for a place that's more sophisticated and cosmopolitan, with more stimulation and warmer weather. I don't mind a rural setting if you have something to go along with it. David is looking for another job again, and a lot depends on where he finds work.

Q: What advice do you have for people who want desperately to move to the country?

A: My advice is to try living in an area for two or three months first, especially if you're used to a faster pace and more mental stimulation. And take some time to experience rural life, rather than a two-week vacation. You should also be careful about burning your bridges behind you.

Maybe you shouldn't make such a drastic transition at first; maybe you should first go to the suburbs from the city, and then to the country, unless you've experienced the country before and know that you can handle it. Or mentally think that you'll do it for two years and then at the end of that time, you have the option to change it. We moved here with the idea that we'd be here for the rest of our lives, which caused even more of a desperate situation for me to get out. If I knew we would be here only a couple of years, it's okay, I can handle that. That's a different mental outlook. Don't say you're doing it for the rest of your life if you don't know if you can or not.

List your expectations, talk to people who have actually done it, and ask if their expectations have been met in the country. Evaluate where are you in your life: maybe the move to the country would not be much of a transition, if your husband has a job and you have small kids. But if you're going to try to find a life for yourself, you may have a more difficult time than you think you would.

I think there's a lot of justification for the trend of people moving to the country and the principles are good, if you can do it in stages or get within 15 minutes of a city and still have a country feeling, you wouldn't feel so isolated.

But there's a lot of value in what actually is taking place, that is, not chasing after prestige, fame and power, but you have to be careful not to go too far the other way, which we definitely did. And I wouldn't recommend that either.

If you have problems dealing with certain issues in the city, you're just going to carry those same problems with you into the country. It doesn't mean that since you're away from certain things that you're not going to have to work out those issues in your own life. Going to the country can solve some problems, but not those that you're dealing with on a personal level. If you're not being fulfilled in one way or another, a move to the country will not be the solution.

Chapter Eight
Odds & Ends

I can't possibly begin to tell you about all the different issues and aspects that will make up your new life in a small town. My experience of moving to northern New England in the late 80s is totally different than if I were to have moved here ten years later, primarily due to the astonishing developments in technology in a very short period of time.

In this chapter, I hope to illuminate some of the things you might encounter about small town life, as well as highlight one area of the country that many people are turning to in order to realize their dreams of living in a place they love.

You have everything you need in order to make the move. So what are you waiting for?

One Woman's Small Town Perspective: Carol Schwartz

My husband and I had been spending summer weekends in Bradford County, Pennsylvania, for eighteen years and had long planned "the big move" from suburban Philadelphia. We felt quite confident and knowledgeable since we had been subscribing to *Country Journal* for decades. Life's unexpected events had delayed the move for many years, so I finally decided on my fiftieth birthday that if I had not moved by my fifty-first, I would abandon that dream and create a new one.

On October 30, 1993, my fifty-first birthday, I was standing on the deck of my new house in the middle of the most beautiful property I have ever seen. That was the good news. The bad news was that it was snowing and we got sixteen inches that day. During that first winter, *sans* central heating, radio or television (that glorious mountain view to the north blocks reception) we were the recipients of one hundred and thirty-two inches of snow. There were many other surprises, some splendid and others not so welcome.

There are many "flatlanders" here, particularly from around Philadelphia, and many have lived in Wellsboro for decades. We joke about what *Country Journal* didn't tell us. The whispered word "Macy's" or, better yet "Clemens" (a fabulous food store chain in the Philadelphia suburbs) evokes in each of these folks a groan and that dreamy, far-away look. We have established a rye bread network; whoever is traveling to a city has to load up for the rest of us. On a trip to Philadelphia in January, having eaten at every ethnic restaurant in my path, I stopped at Clemens on the way home and went straight to the bread counter. It was early in the day and the store was nearly empty. The sight of stacks of rye bread (seeded and unseeded, large and small, sliced and not yet sliced), and *real* pumpernickels and sourdoughs, warmed my heart. I said to the attendant "I would like the rye bread, please." She said, "How many?" I said, "Actually, all of them."

Although, to some degree, we transplants would like the best of both worlds, there have been wonderful tradeoffs. In Philadelphia, I had two teaching jobs, a large Victorian home to tend, full-time graduate work, painting on the side.

Here in a small town I have time for people, time for birds, time to plan and plant fabulous gardens, time to paint and to write. Even time enough to procrastinate and put off until tomorrow most of those things.

Contemplations of living a small town life embody certain myths. We add to that preconceived ideas, certain standards and lots of baggage. Some bear out and some do not. And yes, it does take some time to adjust.

Multiple Occupations

Your first concern about moving to a small town—and perhaps the primary reason why you don't move tomorrow—is probably the lack of a good job. You already know that it will be difficult to find a job that's comparable to the one you have now, so I'll let you in on a little secret that many people in the city and suburbs don't know about small town living.

If you've looked at the Help Wanted ads and wondered how anyone could survive on such abysmally low wages, even when the cost of living is significantly lower, realize this: Most people in a small town do more than one thing to support themselves. And even those who work full-time with decent benefits usually moonlight at something. Often, it's a well-loved hobby that would seem like work if it took up more time.

Here are some examples of people I know: A nurse sells her home-grown potpourri at craft fairs. A woman who works full-time at her husband's satellite dish business also works three nights a week as a waitress in an upscale small town inn, bringing home $80 to $100 each shift. Another is a travel agent who works at home part-time as an instructor in a national correspondence school.

Many of these jobs are seasonal, but some people like to do whatever is in season year-round. It's a good bet that you'll end up working more hours than you did in your city job. However, most people in a small town—both newcomers and natives alike—come to realize that small town life is not about leisure, it's about a lifestyle that's more in keeping with your natural rhythms, which, ironically, may mean more hours spent working, but in a different sense.

Think about flexibility when it comes to multiple occupations. One job could be your mainstay, while another could be in a field that you've always wanted to dabble in. You may also find yourself helping out a neighbor who has a home-based mail order business who has a big rush in December and can give you as much work as you want.

I know hundreds of people in my area, and I can honestly say that only a handful do just one thing to make a living.

You may look around at a small town you have your eye on, and see neighbors with decent houses, nice cars, and nothing shabby about them, even though the husband may just putter around and the wife works as a secretary at the hospital. A couple—or more—sideline jobs are probably the reason why.

Small Town Nicknames

Awhile ago, there was a thread on one of the Internet

rural newsgroups that discussed the nicknames that people living in small towns used to describe people in the city.

Following is a sample of what came up, in addition to some nicknames for small town folk as well:

"I was listening to a story on the radio about two weeks ago. It was a story involving Montana as I remember. One of the locals was talking about all the upscale tourists from the city, and referred to them as the 'cappuccino and Jeep Cherokee' crowd.

"Around here (well, okay, north of here, along the California coastal ranges) a common term of endearment for upscale visitors is 'the scented soap crowd.'"

—*Morgan P.*

"On the central Oregon coast, the tourists are referred to as being 'from town,' meaning Portland, even though it's more than 100 miles away.

"Around Southern Indiana they call small town folk 'hilljacks,' which really confused me the first time I heard it."

—*Derek L.*

"In northern Pennsylvania, it's the ridgerunners (locals) versus the flatlanders (people from away). These are generally *not* terms long-time residents would use. Instead, they would refer to them as 'from down-state,' 'from New Jersey', and so on.

—*A.F.*

"This Massachusetts boy is considered a 'flatlander' by his buddies to the north in Vermont.

—*Steve O.*

"Around here, anyone who wasn't born and raised in the house his father was born and raised in is considered a newcomer. And to my second-generation Ukranian neighbors, anyone who isn't Ukranian is an 'American.' Anyone who isn't a full-time farmer is a yuppie. So even though I have lived on my 11 acres for the last 30 years, I am still all of the above. But fortunately, it is mostly good-natured, and we all get along."

—*Mike S.*

"In this part of North America (Newfoundland), anyone from the capital city is called a 'Townie' while us small town folk are all 'Baymen.'"

—*R.P.*

"My favorite name for city slickers is caged rats, myself included for the moment.
"I find the names given to small town folk more interesting and colorful. These are sure to spark a flame or two, for example: inbreeder, hillbilly, and redneck. I aspire to be called these names some day."

—*Richard H.*

"In coastal Alaska, ya'll are known as 'pukers.' We take you out on fishing boats to catch halibut and salmon, and all you guys do is lean over the rail and chum for sharks (throw up).

"This term is not applied solely to city slickers; it's the generic term for anyone who doesn't live in Alaska year-round."

—*Jan D.*

"Around here, we tell the foreigners by the way they pronounce the town name. They try to say the X and say EX-EENIA or say Zinnia, like the flower.

"It's actually pronounced Zeen-ya by the natives."

—*Corey B.*

"In the southwestern part of Virginia, the way the local folks tell that people are not from here is unique.

"There's a place called 'Dante.' The folks not from around there pronounce it like the poet, as in 'don-tay.'

"It's a hoot whenever a coal strike draws the media from the big cities. The local residents have great sport when the high-powered types ask directions to 'Don-tay.'"

—*Don B.*

"In northern Wisconsin we used to call the Illinois folks that came up north 'flatlanders' and/or 'berrypickers.' I guess they didn't grow any berries in Illinois. Lots of times we just called them 'tourists,' since that just about says it all."

—*Marty J.*

"Here in New England, the term 'Granolas' refers to folks who choose to lead a natural, organic, or earth-friendly lifestyle. It is shortened from 'Granola Munchers,' obviously referring to their dietary preferences.

"I suppose quite a few city-slickers transplanted to small town areas have this attitude, which might be where the usage of the term to describe all city-slickers comes from.

—*Steve O.*

"In Montana, we call them Californians!"

—*Jean M.*

"Born and bred in Indiana, anyone who can call themselves a Hoosier without laughing is a native.

"By the way, when I was in the service, I was returning to base in Colorado from leave when a snowstorm closed I-80, which diverted us down to I-70, which we found out was also closed. We took a motel somewhere in Kansas. I called my commanding officer to inform him that I could not return on schedule due to the snowstorm. He asked where I was.

"'Gosh, I'm in the middle of absolutely nothing! Some Podunk town named...(I forgot).'

"There was dead silence.

"Then came his reply, 'My wife and I grew up in that town!' A classic case of foot-in-mouth disease."

—*Rose I.*

Lawn Mowers Anonymous

"We want shaven carpets of grass here and there, but what nonsense it is to shave it as often as foolish men shave their faces!"
William Robinson
The Wild Garden, 1894

With a suburban or urban home, maintaining your lawn is undoubtedly a necessity. With a house in a small town, however, you have a bit more flexibility as to what to do with your lawn. Unless you use the art of lawnmowing as a way to meditate or just relax, consider going without an elaborate front lawn at your new home in a small town.

At my house high up on a hill, the summer sun beats down relentlessly and the standard grade of lawn seed the previous owner tossed around is a thirsty breed. Given the combination of a long, dry summer with a well that wouldn't sustain an extended session with a lawnsprinkler, I've had to lug out the lawnmower to wrestle the non-bald spots on my half-acre of cleared land only twice, on average, per summer.

Why not give it up completely? This summer, I'm going to stand on my deck and toss handfuls of wildflower seeds over the railing after the first heavy early-June rain, just to see what takes root.

If you're interested in forgoing a lawn when you

move to a small town, here are some resources:

Books
The Wild Lawn Handbook: Alternatives to the Traditional Front Lawn, by Stevie Daniels. Published by Macmillan, 1995.

Mail-order Sources
Applewood Seed Company
POB 10761
Golden CO 80401
303-431-6283

Ernst Crownvetch Farms
RD 5 Box 806
Meadville PA 16335
800-873-3321

Niche Gardens
1111 Dawson Road
Chapel Hill NC 27516
919-967-0078

Vermont Wildflower Farm
Route 7 Box 5
Charlotte VT 05445
802-425-3931

Prairie Restorations
POB 327
Princeton MN 55371
612-389-4342

Organizations
American Floral Meadow Society
C/o John Krouse

University of Maryland
Cherry Hill Turf Research Facility
3120 Gracefield Rd
Silver Spring MD 20904
301-572-7247

Backyard Wildlife Habitat Program
National Wildlife Federation
1400 16th St NW
Washington DC 20036

National Wildflower Research Center
2600 FM 973 North
Austin TX 78725
512-929-3600

New England Wildflower Society
Garden in the Woods
Hemenway Road
Framingham MA 01701
508-237-4924

The North Country Report

If you're thinking about moving to the north country
in the eastern part of the United States, you may be
surprised to discover that each state has its own
unique identity that is hard to uncover if you're just
passing through on vacation or a short visit.

I'm not talking about Vermont and maple syrup
and Maine and lighthouses, I'm referring to the more
esoteric differences in attitudes among the people who
live there. Yes, some of the people you'll encounter
will seem like walking stereotypes of a person who

walked right off a poster from the state tourism agency, but the subtleness is much more personal, and it takes time to discover.

Of course, many people from away already realize this, as they're drawn to a particular state and no other. Whether or not you're still pondering the best state for you to move to, or you've already made up your mind, what you're about to read should prove illuminating at the very least.

What It's Like to Live in Maine

Maine has not one but *two* identities and two different worlds: the coast, and inland. At times, it may seem like you're living in two states in one, or only half a state, depending on how you see it.

If you know you want to move to Maine, chances are you know if you prefer the coast or inland, where some parts are flat while others—especially in western Maine—are mountainous. Unlike Vermont and New Hampshire, most of Maine has the reputation of being fairly rural and pretty far removed from cosmopolitan influences, primarily because it's so big. There is a lot of culture in many small Maine towns, since the people in the community are basically responsible for developing and maintaining any semblance of the arts if they want to have any at all. This is one reason why the state continues to draw people from away to push its population over the one million mark.

Once you get a bit north of the crowded Portland area, most of the state is rural. And even where it's not—like Augusta, the state capitol, or Bangor, home to Stephen King—chances are that if you head a mile out of town in any direction, you'll hit farms and dirt roads in short order. Even in the bustling tourist metropolises around Kennebunk and Saco in southern Maine, the same rules apply, except that encroaching suburbia is also very much in evidence.

One thing I love about Maine are the hundreds of towns that are unnamed, but the state government had to do something to delineate each of these mostly uninhabited 36-square-mile towns, so it granted each a complex number and letter name. What's particularly compelling about them is that some of these townships are within a two-hour drive of Portland. Look at a map, and you'll see that a high percentage of the state's land mass consists of these unincorporated townships. Besides the letter-and-number combination, some have interesting names, like Big 20 Township at the very northern tip of Maine to Misery Township, Lower Enchanted Township, and even Dallas Pit.

The bad thing about Maine is that it can get very crowded in the summertime. Unlike New Hampshire or Vermont, where the tourism is spread out a little bit more throughout the year, after Labor Day in Maine, things just about die—on the ocean, at least. Most people—especially tourists—don't like the ocean in winter. Inland, however, is another story because of the mountains and Sugarloaf in the Carrabassett Valley and Sunday River in Bethel, as well as a wealth of smaller ski areas that are scattered around the western part of the state.

Here, then, some of my impressions based on recent ramblings through the Pine Tree State.

The environs around Brunswick appeal to many aspiring Mainiacs—yes that's what you'll be called as a resident—because of the presence of Bowdoin College and the proximity of the ocean and nearby islands. Old New England architecture also abounds in this area, however, with real estate prices to match. You'll find that the cost of identical houses—one on the coast and the other ten miles inland—will be significantly different. And 50 miles inland, the difference is even more striking.

No matter. As in the western part of the United States, since Maine as a state is so big, driving 50 miles in an area with no rush hour traffic is not the heart-pounding anxiety-ridden adventure you've probably come to associate with it. Of course, you should keep in mind that in any rural area, you'll have to get used to driving farther for opportunities, whether they're for work or a performance of La Boheme. But keep in mind that up here, people hibernate all winter, venturing out only for certain necessary occasions--which can include a dose of culture.

In fact, the great thing about so much of the coast in Maine is that it is so rural, with old farmhouses, dirt roads and cellar holes scattered at what goes for densely populated up here. And this becomes more of a factor the further north you get. For instance, in the town of Brooksville, 20 miles up the coast from Belfast on the Blue Hill peninsula, there is an old general store with a lunch counter in the back which serves as the central focus of the village and the main gathering place for the people, and there are miles of paved, winding roads with dirt roads that shoot off from it.

Here are my observations of a few towns based on my visits there:

Kents Hill, near Livermore Falls, about 25 miles west of Augusta, is located in what is called the Lakes Region of the state. I must say that this area is even too rural and remote for me, which is saying a lot;

and you wouldn't necessarily pick up on it by looking at a map, either. Probably because a century or two ago, the area was bustling, and as I wandered around the town, I saw lots of cellar holes, abandoned houses, and roads that led nowhere. That kind of northern New England town where the reverence for past history is more palpable than the influence of the 20th century spooks me somewhat and that's probably why I felt that way about the area.

In fact, in Livermore Falls is the sole attraction in town called Norlands Living History Center, a 450-acre living history complex where you can experience what it was like to live in the late 1800s in this area of Maine.

Hallowell, right outside Augusta, on the other hand, holds lots of government job opportunities, relatively speaking, and there are many rural areas, but it had the kind of feel to it with new modular homes plopped down in the subdivided middle of what used to be a field that you know any undeveloped parcel won't remain like that for long.

Up on Mount Desert Island and near Bar Harbor, the islands are exceedingly pretty, less rural than I'd like it, and crowded.

I've never been to Camden, but from what I've been told, it's a magnet for people from away to settle. One couple I know lived in York, in southern Maine, for a few years, but they found the people to be provincial and thought they didn't strive enough. "The next year, they'll still be stuck in the same place, talking about the same things they were talking about a year ago," said the woman. So they moved to Camden, which has a slightly cosmopolitan flavor to it, even though ruralness lies less than a mile beyond the main village.

For some reason, every town named Washington is pretty desolate, and Maine is no exception. Washington is 15 miles west of Camden as the crow flies.

Washington County, which touches Canada, is also pretty desolate, and even though I prefer the mountains to the ocean, and truthfully, Washington County is far more remote and underpopulated than Lincoln County, where Kents Hill and Livermore Falls are located, I liked Washington County better. And I can't put my finger on it, except to say that Washington County is so far removed from the commonly traveled areas of Maine that it remains mostly untouched by tourism and people who just dabble in rural living. This is the real thing. But you'd better know what you're doing if you move all the way up here, because the winters are long and there aren't many attractions or industry to speak of. In fact, the Canadian influence here is significant, since Campobello Island—in Canada—sits just off the coast from Lubec, in Maine, and less than 30 miles from Machias, the county seat of Washington County.

Oxford is located in the western part of the state. I've sensed that these inland areas tend to be more conservative in nature than the coast. This makes sense, since many newcomers—from traditionally liberal areas like New York and Boston—are mainly attracted to and have the money to live on the coast, while some seventh generation members of old, staid Maine families never budged from the original family grants. Even though it's relatively near a major tourist attraction—30 miles from Bethel and the Sunday River ski area—Oxford is like that. There are a number of small family farms scattered around the area; at one, the family grows fruits and vegetables on ten acres of farmland in summer and runs a cross-country ski center over those same fields in winter, in addition to operating a B&B year-round.

There are a growing number of people from away who are eschewing the coast of Maine and settling on the extreme west central part of the state, the area that includes Fryeburg, Sebago Lake, Poland Spring, and all of those towns named after foreign countries and cities: Norway, South Paris, Denmark, Poland, and Naples. Why this area? It's a relatively straight shot to Portland, 45 miles away, but it also borders the area around North Conway, New Hampshire, home of no sales tax and outlet shopping galore, not to mention some significant employment, both seasonal and year-round. This area of the state, however, is also a strong area for tourism--but again, mostly in the summer. The canoe outfitters in Fryeburg that send thousands of tourists down the Saco River each year, employ hundreds of people. The businesses in North Conway employ thousands.

Bethel also has a sizable industry which is not initially apparent from its first impressions. There's Gould Academy, a prep school, and several large farms and lumber mills. And yes, the industry that supports Sunday River—which is technically in the town of Newry—is sizable as well.

Keep heading north along the New Hampshire border and you'll reach the Rangeley/Sugarloaf area, which is a bit of an oasis out in the middle of nowhere. Again, much of the area's industry and employment opportunities revolve around the ski area.

Then starting at around 70 miles north of Bangor on I-95, as you'd expect, the area is more unpopulated—you may recognize the names Millinocket and Baxter State Park—but the major industry from here west to the New Hampshire border is lumber. One estimate puts the number of acres with population in the North Woods at 6.5 million, with no public roads running through them, only logging roads. Logging trucks pretty much rule the roads up here. That and hunting lodges and resorts—with no phone lines, you reach them by radio phone since the cost of putting in telephone lines would be prohibitive—and some of the places are so remote that you have to fly in to get to them or else ferry across one of the lakes. Me, I can't see why anyone would want to live so far removed from civilization—even though there are many people who already put me in that category, since I live 20 miles from an Interstate exit and 30 miles from a fast-food restaurant—but many of the people who have moved to Maine's North Woods are in the hospitality business, where they are able to have contact with other people, and so they don't go too crazy from the lack of contact.

I've heard people describe the state as having many different Maines. After traveling extensively throughout the state, I can say that each town is a different Maine. And whether it's ocean or mountain you want, there's a lot in Maine. You just have to travel a bit to find it. And just as most of Canada's population lives within 100 miles of the American border, the majority of Mainiacs live within 10 miles of the Atlantic Ocean.

What It's Like to Live in New Hampshire

Not too long ago, I listened to a national radio broadcast where the topic was why New Hampshire is the only state in the nation to vote against having a

Martin Luther King Jr. holiday.

"We look at it this way," said the commentator. "It doesn't have much to do with racism. Take our neighboring states: Vermont is known as being cute, and well, *Vermonty*. Maine has the ocean. Both have great images in the public eye of the tourist. What does New Hampshire have? Granite. That and the stubbornness of the people. We don't want to foster a one-dimensional stereotype about the state like Maine or Vermont does, and we don't want to feel like we're being pressured into anything.

"Everyone else is pushing New Hampshire to approve the King holiday," he continued, "but many staunch conservatives in the legislature feel that if they succumb to the pressure, then the state will just be like everyone else. At least this sets them apart."

A curious explanation, to be sure, but an accurate one nonetheless. Live Free or Die is the best motto for a state where there is no state zoning—like in Vermont—and no state income or sales tax. People move to New Hampshire from cities and suburbs because they want to live independent lives, and not because they want to be known as Vermonters or Mainiacs.

And other New Hampshirites/Granite Staters are quite content to let you be--until you need help, that is, when they're at your side in a flash. This characteristic is largely indicative of rural life as a whole, but I think the extremes are more pronounced in New Hampshire due to that fierce independent streak that seems to dominate everything else.

Don't let the ultra-conservative tone of the *Union-Leader*, the state's largest daily newspaper, fool you. Read between the lines, and you'll see that it's really yet another example of the overriding desire of people in the state to Live Free or Die.

I love living in New Hampshire. When I first moved to a small town in northern New England, I used to say I would have an 802 (Vermont) area code for the rest of my life, but that changed a few years ago. First of all, so many people—visitors and residents alike—ooh and aah over the image that is Vermont, that it gets tiring if you live there and are constantly exposed to it. Not to mention the hordes of tourists. I always wanted to move to the country to get away from the crowds, not to encounter them whenever I need to pick up a newspaper. And when something in Vermont is cute or quaint, it's really cute or quaint. Just look at the color photos in *Vermont Life*; colors like that don't occur naturally.

Vermont and New Hampshire have long been compared to each other, with New Hampshire usually getting the short end of the stick. That's too bad. I once had a woman who lives in northwestern Vermont snap at me because of what she perceived to be a lack of state-funded social services in New Hampshire compared to Vermont, and this was because I just happen to live in New Hampshire. This seems to be a common personality trait when you cross the Connecticut River.

A word about New Hampshire schools. There is currently a huge war being fought over the issue of how the state should fund education. In late 1993, the current system of relying primarily on property taxes was found to be unconstitutional, since towns with a higher tax base—many are ski towns with fewer children and therefore a higher amount is spent on each student—can fund more than poorer towns which typically have more children in the schools. And in a state with no income tax and no sales tax, this means that the property taxes are usually exorbitantly high. But compare them with Vermont's, which are usually higher.

There are many regional high school districts which take students from a number of surrounding towns. Most towns follow the same formula, with one central school pulling in students from up to seven or more different neighboring towns. My feeling is that if you can move to a town where at least one or two of the included towns tend to be wealthier, then the school will benefit, and so will your kids.

Anyway, here's a rundown of the rural areas of New Hampshire. I'll automatically rule out the southeast area that includes Manchester and Nashua, and also the seacoast; the former because these are basically suburban bedroom communities of Boston, the latter because the area from Seabrook north to Portsmouth is heavily populated.

The Monadnock Region

This southwest corner of the state, which includes Keene, Walpole and Peterborough—is among the least-traveled areas of the state, as well as one of the most community-minded. Keene State College is a major employer and cultural draw, and several medical centers are in the area. The nearby town of Rindge has Franklin Pierce College, and Hinsdale has a racetrack. Other than that, the remaining rural towns in the area, which include Alstead and Washington to the north, and Troy and Winchester to the south, are pretty, though utilitarian working-class towns. Jaffrey and Dublin, to the east of Keene, are old-moneyed, elegant towns with many grand 200-year-old houses.

On the whole, the Monadnock region is quiet and unassuming, and it would be easy to settle into one of the outlying towns, but you would definitely be noticed.

Concord & the Capital Region

As with many rural states, it seems that if you get five miles outside of the capital, you'll hit rural land. Concord is no exception. Such towns as Weare, Northwood, Henniker and Warner, all within a 20-minute drive of Concord, are rural areas with strong local economic bases, which means the residents don't have to drive far for work. Route 4 that runs through Northwood is known as Antique Alley; there is a sizable summer population here as well. Henniker is home to New England College, and both Weare and Warner have a large number of local businesses.

Concord itself empties out after 6 p.m.; it's up to the surrounding towns to provide the entertainment, at which, between the college and the close-knit communities, they largely succeed. Also, the fact that the area is less than a two-hour drive to Boston makes it easy to make day trips for a large dose of culture and civilization.

The Upper Valley

The Upper Valley is the central area of the twin-state region of New Hampshire and Vermont. The New Hampshire side is home to Dartmouth College; everything in the area pretty much revolves around the college and the Dartmouth-Hitchcock Medical Center, which employs 5000 people alone. There are also a number of thriving theatre groups and state-financed readings and discussions in the outlying towns, however, since many people who work in Hanover and

Lebanon choose to live outside of these towns.

My town, Grafton, is on the eastern outskirts of the Upper Valley just before the Lakes Region begins. There's no tourism here to speak of—and therefore no crowds—and people pretty much pass through town on their way to someplace else. If you crave isolation—and remember, this is New Hampshire, where no one is going to talk to you unless you talk to them first—a town like Grafton would be a good choice for you. But if you want a little bit more activity, a town that has more people than Grafton's 800 and is closer to cultural outposts like Hanover, would be better for you.

You'll pay for the convenience, however. A 7-room farmhouse on one acre in town sold for $35,000 in 1995. Even in Canaan, the next town over, with a population of over 2000, you can't find something like that.

The Lakes Region

This section, which encompasses Bristol to the west, Campton to the north, the Maine border to the east, and Laconia to the south, is a prime area for tourists. The Lakes Region can be as gaudy as New Year's Eve, and as pristine as the scenery in the movie On Golden Pond, which was filmed on Squam Lake in Holderness. Plymouth State College is a major hub, but there isn't much industry to speak of besides tourism, which goes way beyond peak in the summertime.

Meredith, Weirs Beach and Gilford may remind you of the Jersey shore--instead check out the towns of Sandwich, Hebron and Moultonborough if you're looking for a real rural area.

The White Mountains

This is the area that most people get their impressions of New Hampshire from; given its development and also its diversity, it's a pretty accurate picture.

North Conway, Jackson, Lincoln, and Waterville Valley are the major towns that are busy winter and summer. There are plenty of businesses oriented towards tourism as well as some light manufacturing and business service companies, started by many of the former urbanites who moved to the White Mountains and brought their companies with them—or started one so that they could stay.

Traffic jams on Route 16 in North Conway are legendary due to the vast array of outlet shops and other stores, and can come to an absolute standstill on Route 3 passing by the Old Man of the Mountains. But aside from traffic, most parts of the White Mountains are undeveloped, majestic lands and make any inconvenience worth it.

The Nether Regions

Look at a map of New Hampshire. At Littleton on the northwest border, cut a line straight across and look at the area that lies north of the line. There's a town called Stark about an hour northeast of Littleton. The name of that town pretty much characterizes the entire area.

Berlin, on the eastern side of the area, is the largest town in what I call the Nether Regions. It has 13,000 people and a 100,000-watt radio station, and not much else compared to the rest of the state. It's not too often that a person will move to this area without family contacts. It's tough to live up here—

the winters last about a month longer than areas further south, and the landscape is more desolate. The main attractions of the White Mountain National Forest are south of the line, and though the towns of Jefferson and Dixville Notch have some tourist attractions, there's not much going on. Many of the people make their living from the woods or by holding onto three or four different seasonal jobs throughout the year.

Because it's tough up here, the locals will question your motives in moving there. I've heard that except in the major towns like Littleton and Berlin, natives look particularly askance at newcomers.

It's also impossible to get there from here in a straight line, since only a few state highways service the area.

Moving to the country is a drastic-enough change for most people. Best not to make it so drastic that you give up early.

What It's Like to Live in Upstate New York

I'll warn you now so it doesn't catch you by surprise later on: After you move to a rural area of New York State, if you travel across state lines for any amount of time, people are going to think you're from The City and automatically jump to conclusions about you. No matter how hard you may work at disassociating yourself from your urban past, you won't ever be able to totally escape it. As they say up in my neck of the woods, once a flatlander, always a flatlander.

You can dispel those rumors and tell them that most of New York State is exceedingly rural and even wilderness, but they won't listen. So just be prepared.

Some people feel that the minute that you get on the New York State Thruway and hit the 914 area code, they are leaving city life behind, but of course, it's not that easy. For that, you'll have to head up to the area north of White Plains on the east side of the Hudson River and beyond Spring Valley on the west before you can truly feel that you're in the country. Of course, many people will choose to keep going, some for hundreds of miles north and/or west.

Rural New York State is largely unappreciated as a good place to live. Yes, it's cheaper, but many people feel that as long as they're going to head north, then Vermont or some other New England state is *it* for them, since New York State doesn't have the cachet of Vermont, the otherworldliness of New Hampshire, or the cragginess of Maine.

If you choose New York State, however, there are real benefits. For one, once you get north and/or west of Albany, the prices on real estate and the cost of living begin to drop precipitiously. In fact, the prices along the eastern border of Adirondack State Park are incredibly low in the small towns and villages, again because I've found that many people who choose to live in this area and this far north would rather call themselves Vermonters and live across Lake Champlain and pay real estate prices that are at least double for a comparable house. In New York State, at least, you have the view of Vermont, as well as easy access.

But besides the eastern Adirondacks, New York State is filled with rural enclaves, some extremely backwater, others quite cosmopolitan. Here, then, are some tidbits about selected towns all over the state.

The lower New York State Thruway corridor begins just about at Newburgh and environs and continues until you reach the northern parallel of Catskill Park. There's a lot of diversity and industry in this area, from SUNY at New Paltz to the overrated Woodstock and the quaint—but expensive—Rhinebeck.

There are jobs to be found--as in many areas that are favored by escaped urbanites, as this place is. Since the distance from New York City ranges from less than an hour in this region to 90 minutes away, the disadvantage of living in this area is that you may still feel like you're in the city at times. For some pewople, this might be just the security blanket they need, while for others, however, it won't do the trick. If you're in this latter category, keep the car pointed north.

And so, north of this area, you start to enter into modified rural suburbia 20 miles before you reach Albany. You don't want this, so again, keep going. But you might want to check out the area that's west of Newburgh that runs to the east and northern border of Pennsylvania. This is rural life incarnate—the only populated drawing card is Monticello; otherwise, farms, desolation and large rickety tourist hotels are the norm. This little corner of New York State is quite far removed from easy access to the city and to Albany, which means it's pretty much stood still in terms of development.

Along the corridor of I-88 that runs from Schnectady to Binghamton, the most famous rural town in this region—and one that you've probably visited or at least been dragged to—is Cooperstown. I remember that when I drove there several years ago, I couldn't help but marvel at all of the ramshackle, beatup little towns we drove through to get there. I hadn't realized that this central area of the state was so depressed, and yes, it is possible to buy a real house here for $15,000, but you probably wouldn't want to live here, simply because it is *too* depressed.

Within ten miles of Cooperstown, as is the case on your approach to any big city, the landscape and the flavor of the area begin to change. Things begin to look a little more spruced up, and if you're coming in at night, you see the faint glow sit low in the sky like some kind of itinerant flying saucer hovering just above the earth, and the houses and the people both begin to look well-scrubbed. Then you hit the town, and it's some oasis—depending upon your view—out in the middle of nowhere, with a bit of the carnival atmosphere to it. Not too long ago, someone ventured that he thought I would enjoy living in Cooperstown. Wrong person, I said, not even within 25 miles.

An aside here: there are many main highways that crisscross the state that allow people to travel to major areas and get to neighboring states pretty directly. You're never too far from an interstate highway or a good-sized state highway in New York, which means that many of the people who have moved to rural New York State from other parts of the state need to work for themselves because there's just not much else there. So you'll find many of these transplants make things a bit easier. This is a starting point when it comes to job hunting, that is, approach small businesses looking for work, but it's also where you'll find many cultural events centered, since these people brought their tastes with them in the 60s and 70s during the last nationwide bolt to the country. Some left after their first stab at communal living and organic farming, but some stayed behind, altering their country environs to suit their lives. So if you want to use this as a benchmark for scouting out different areas in the state and re not particularly picky about the area or town, try it as a testing ground.

I'm personally not familiar with much of New York State that starts on the southern parallel of Adirondack State Park and heads north. However, I gather from friends who have visited or lived in the area that there truly is not much to speak of in the way of employment or attractions, save for the areas around Lake Placid, Lake George, and the desolate peace of the Park itself. In other words, this is a great place to be a loner, if you do indeed lean towards this. You could easily get lost living in the park with little human contact. I do, however, assume that my readers don't want to become absolute hermits, other- wise, they would have left the city and suburbs years, even decades ago to live in a grumpy old shack in the middle of nowhere.

Where it gets interesting, as far as a rural place to live, is the panhandle of the state, west of I-81 from roughly Binghamton in the south to Syracuse in the north, and then all the way west, to Buffalo. When lifelong New York Staters think about the areas in the state where the people are the most backwoods, they usually point to the panhandle—which also contains the Finger Lakes region—long before they'd point to the Adirondacks. If you look at a map, you'll see that this area of the state appears to be more developed than the Adirondack State Park area, but while the 'dack's main feature is wilderness, the panhandle area contains a number of strange little towns that are surrounded by rural areas, while still remaining rela- tively close to major league towns like Jamestown, Batavia and Elmira.

Here, then, are some of the more quirky towns in this region:

Seneca Falls and its rural environs, just west of Auburn on Route 20, was home to Elizabeth Cady Stanton, America's first feminist. Accordingly, the area remains a mecca for feminists and a large PC women's community. The National Women's Hall of Fame is located here as well as the Seneca Falls Women's Rights National Historical Park. Many people would be turned off by this blinders-on devotion by a sizable part of the town, and the truth is that there are minor skirmishes between the more conservative citizens and the women's community, but others pay it no mind.

The sleepy town of Angelica, which isn't near a thing except other towns just like it, is in Allegany County, a region that's filled with back-to-the-landers—both people who have chosen it as a way of life as well as natives who don't know how to live any other way. These people truly do live off the land, and consider hunting season to last twelve months out of the year.

Among Angelica's distinctions are the following: it successfully fought off the state government's desire to place a low-level radioactive waste site in the town. The town also won the distinction of having the best water in the state in 1988. If you think that other urbanites wouldn't be attracted to an area this far west or so filled with homesteaders of all stripes, think again. Back in the mid-80s, a couple from Long Island picked Angelica as a place to settle and opened the Angelica Inn. If you visit the town and stay at the inn, ask them why they picked Angelica.

When people in Buffalo decide they want to move to the country, they head 15 miles southeast of

Buffalo to East Aurora. The village proper fairly bustles and contains a National Historic District. Once home to Millard Fillmore, East Aurora is perfect for aspiring ruralites who want to become familiar with village life but don't want to cut the umbilical cord to the city just yet. But you should forget about East Aurora if you're allergic to winter.

Geneseo, in the center of the panhandle, will be the most attractive town profiled here to some people for a variety of reasons. Number 1: it's a college town—with SUNY at Geneseo—and as I've learned from experience, proximity to a college town makes the occasional *So now what should we do's?* more tolerable, especially during the long northern winters. The town is also a stone's throw from I-390, which makes for convenience. However, it's also a pretty straight shot of 30 miles into Rochester, where it's easy to get your city dose, but you can also feel great about leaving it behind and not having to drive for several hours to reach your country home.

Geneseo is exceedingly rural, with plenty of gently rolling hills and valleys that define the region. The town is also pretty diverse with not only the university, but a nearby monastery, farmers, professors, an old-money population, and what we in New Hampshire call woodchucks but the rest of the country calls rednecks. It's a neat area with lots of pluses, to be sure.

Lastly, if you're like me and appreciate being able to travel easily to another country—in this case, Canada—then try Westfield, the westernmost New York town on the Thruway before you reach Pennsylvania, where just across Lake Erie in Ontario.

There are a number of vineyards in and around the countryside of Westfield, and the proximity to the lake allows for higher temperatures and therefore a longer growing season. And there are lots of abandoned houses—and breweries—in this region, which adds to that end-of-the-world mystique. If you're looking for a congenial small town with a typical Main Street, Westfield is it, with old brick buildings that house diners, hardware stores and lots of antiques shops.

The best thing I can tell you about finding the best place for you to live in New York State is to get in the car and spend as much time as possible wandering around. New York State is so huge, and its various towns are so different from one another—even if they're adjacent to each other--that you really can't tell unless you spend some time there. Stay in a small inn or B&B if you can. As is the case with Angelica, the majority of B&B owners and innkeepers moved from somewhere else—usually downstate—and can give you a pretty accurate thumbnail sketch of what life would be like as a newcomer to their area.

What It's Like to Live in Vermont

Both the media and the state itself do a wonderful job when it comes to making people ooh and aah over the Green Mountain State and make them want to live there.

As with any dream, however, the fantasy usually doesn't match the reality, and usually some adjustments are necessary once you realize this.

But it's no big deal; just that living in Vermont will expose you to far more than spending a few vacation days in Manchester or Stowe will.

I've lived in three different towns in Vermont:

Barnard, South Pomfret, and Norwich, all in the Upper Valley area near Dartmouth. I've also written a travel guide to Vermont, which had me driving all over the state one summer. As a result, I've developed a love-hate relationship with the state. On the one hand, it is a gorgeous state. On the other, I always got the feeling that Vermont never lets you forget that you're living in Vermont. In other words, it sometimes felt like I was living in a postcard, Greetings from the Green Mountain State. Now, how much that has to do with my early impressions of Vermont—drummed into me by the media—when I was still living in New York that if you're going to move to the country, no self-respecting New Yorker would move anywhere but Vermont—and how much of that is due to my impressions of the state's people after I moved, I'm not sure. But if you want to see a Vermonter's hackles rise, just ask him about New Hampshire. It's almost as if they've been slapped. Noses go up in the air, superiority about Vermont's social service system, and the careful zoning in Vermont, which has backfired in recent years. Ask ten different people about Act 250—the statewide zoning law—and you'll get ten different responses.

Daily life, of course, will depend on what you're doing for work, whether you live in one of the state's cities, villages, or out on a back road five miles from town. As in many rural towns, there's a general store, post office, and perhaps a gas station with a small— less than 2000—population, with one exception. Even in the most remote parts of the state, there will be plenty of out-of-state cars parked outside with its occupants inside perusing the Vermont Products section in the general store.

The state's tourism department has done a superb

job in marketing Vermont as a destination where people in overpopulated urban and suburban areas can come to slow down and catch a glimpse of "the way it used to be." And certainly, some of these general stores look like they haven't been touched since 1901.

Fortunately, this revenue from visitors helps the local economy and provides jobs—albeit a lot of low-paying ones—for people who might not be able to stay in Vermont otherwise. However, since many people want to move to a rural area to escape these very crowds, newcomers who expect Vermont to be a pristine, underpopulated state may be in for a surprise.

Because more than half the state population consists of people who have moved to Vermont in the last twenty years, there are plenty of people there who can give you advice on how to move—just stop in one of the shops in Manchester or Stowe and ask how *they* did it. However, I must warn you that some of these people subscribe to the last-one-in closed gate theory; right after they moved to Vermont, they decided it would be best if no one else moved there, so they automatically treat aspiring newcomers with disdain. However, these people are the exception.

I'll chop Vermont up into what amounts to six sections: Southwest; Southeast; West Central; East Central; Northwest; and Northeast.

Southwest

Bennington is the largest city in this area, with Manchester to the north close behind. Bennington is a college town while Manchester is a ski town. The towns located immediately outside of each are decidedly the more rural areas in this section.

If you've spent much time in the central or northern sections of the state, the flatness of Bennington and the towns that run north from it up to Manchester may seem like they're not really part of Vermont. This is the Taconic Valley, and has it lots of fertile farmland, but not much in the way of mountains, unless you get a few towns east of Bennington and into the foothills of the Green Mountains.

Manchester offers more jobs than Bennington or elsewhere in the southwest, but the ones that are easiest to get are connected with the tourist industry, as is the case with most of the state, except Burlington, in the northwest part of Vermont.

Southeast

The southeast section, which runs from Vernon in the extreme southeast corner, west to Whitingham, north to Ludlow, and east to Ascutney, is an area that incorporates counterculture that's alive and well in Brattleboro and Putney, genteel and expensive country in Grafton and Newfane, raucous ski country of Mount Snow in Dover and Stratton in Bondville, and the old bustling factory town of Springfield.

Because of this diversity, there is nothing to distinguish the southeast corner except its diversity. It's said that some newcomers settle in this area because once they cross over the border into Vermont on I-91, they're so happy they're finally in the state that they stop right where they are.

There seems to be an abundance of small office businesses in the area, which sometimes warrant employing locals. I've also heard of a number of people who commute to Boston or New York once a week for work. This area is less glamorous than those farther north, but the housing prices also reflect this—an old farmhouse on a few acres can be found for less than $75,000 in many parts of the area.

East Central

From Windsor northwest to Bridgewater, then north to Randolph and northeast up to Wells River, is the trapezoidal area known as the Vermont side of the Upper Valley, an area distinguished by Dartmouth College on the New Hampshire side of the Connecticut River, and Woodstock in Vermont.

Much of this area contains small, once-bustling hill towns like Tunbridge, Corinth, and Thetford. Granite quarries and sawmills were once the biggest industries; now, people tend to commute to work—some to the White River Junction/Lebanon, New Hampshire, area, others to Barre or Montpelier, which offer more jobs in a concentrated area than does the southern part of the region.

There are still many farms and old-timers in the area. Elementary schools tend to be small—the last one-room schoolhouses closed in Pomfret only a few years ago--and the area's cultural hotbeds are White River Junction, Woodstock, and Randolph.

I-89 snakes its way through the East Central section, but on the whole, the area is relatively peaceful and very rural.

West Central

North of Manchester up to Addison, northeast to Montpelier and south to Brookfield is the West Central section of Vermont. The western border, which borders Lake Champlain, is surprisingly flat for Vermont—many large farms are found in communities like Shoreham and Orwell.

Middlebury College is one of the focal points of the area, along with Rutland, which with its strip malls and sprawling commercial areas, sometimes doesn't seem to be part of Vermont.

Follow Route 100 and you'll be driving through the Green Mountain range, through Killington and Pico Peak.

Jobs are most plentiful in Rutland, although the towns of Waitsfield and Warren, where the Sugarbush ski area is located, are bustling winter and summer. Montpelier and Barre have a large concentration of industries—Montpelier has a bohemian flavor while Barre, home to the largest granite quarry in the country, tends more towards the working class.

Northwest

Burlington, the largest city in the state and home to seven colleges, is the focal point of the northwest corner as well as the entire state, in the opinions of some people. Surrounding communities such as Shelburne, Winooski, Williston and Colchester, are largely suburban. Rural areas are found in Huntington, Underhill, and Cambridge, and housing tends to be priced higher here than elsewhere in the state. A multitude of jobs is the reason why, though Burlington's crime rate has risen in the last few years.

Elsewhere in the area is Stowe with its ski area, Montgomery, a rural outpost of old hippies, craggy natives, and idealistic newcomers, and St. Albans, a sizable city—for Vermont, that is—with an old architectural downtown. The island towns in Lake Champlain—Alburg, Hero and Isle LaMotte—are an entire world within themselves, as is any island community with a curious amalgam of year-round loners.

Northeast

Compared to the rest of Vermont, the Northeast Kingdom, as this part of the state is referred to, is pioneer country. I'd estimate that this one-fifth of the state's land mass holds about 8 percent of the people. A number of Northeast Kingdom towns are named but unorganized, with populations in the single digits, if that.

Many newcomers settle in the picturesque towns of Peacham, Barnet, and East Burke, which has a perennially-struggling ski area. St. Johnsbury is the main city in the area, and nearby Lyndon has a state college.

People in the extreme northeast corner—which includes the towns of Canaan, Island Pond, and Bloomfield—say they feel more of an affinity with New Hampshire than Vermont, since the Vermont papers arrive here the next day, and the TV and radio stations are from New Hampshire and Canada.

But besides the beautiful, often desolate land up here, that's about all you'll find here. When I've visited, I've felt the people up here are not as suspicious of newcomers as those in the rest of the state. Unlike the extreme northern part of New Hampshire, where the people look with wary eyes at newcomers, in Vermont, where it's just as much of a challenge to get through the winter, the people take more of a "the more the merrier, we're in this together" attitude, even though neighbors can sometimes be few and far between.

Index